JONAH

JONAH
A Handbook on the Hebrew Text

W. Dennis Tucker, Jr.

Baylor University Press
Waco, Texas USA

Book Design by Diane Smith
Cover Design by Pam Poll
Cover photograph by Bruce and Kenneth Zuckerman, West Semitic Research, in collaboration with the ancient Biblical Manuscript Center. Courtesy Russina National Library (Saltykov-Shchedrin).

Library of Congress Cataloging-in-Publication Data

Tucker, W. Dennis.
   Jonah : a handbook on the Hebrew text / W. Dennis Tucker, Jr.
       p. cm. -- (Baylor handbook on the Hebrew Bible series)
   Text of Jonah in Hebrew with English translation; commentary in English.
   Includes bibliographical references and index.
   ISBN-13: 978-1-932792-66-9 (pbk. : alk. paper)
   1. Bible. O.T. Jonah--Commentaries. I. Bible. O.T. Jonah. English. Tucker. 2006. II. Bible. O.T. Jonah. Hebrew. 2006. III. Title.

BS1605.53.T83 2006
224'.92044--dc22
                              2006025655

Printed in the United States of America on acid-free paper with a minimum of 30% pcw recycled content.

Baylor Handbook on the Hebrew Bible Series

General Editor

W. Dennis Tucker, Jr.

To Hannah, Sarah,
and Hope

TABLE OF CONTENTS

PREFACE

The story of Jonah was one of the first stories I remember hearing as a child, and the complexity of the book was lost on the simplicity of the story. As an adult, however, and one living in the midst of increasing globalization, the simplicity of the story seems lost on the complexity of the story and its "prophetic" message. The complexity of the story is experienced even further as one makes her or his way through the Hebrew text, noting the frequent word plays, diverse rhetorical devices, and various syntactic constructions. In preparing this handbook, I have been reminded of the joy of reading the Hebrew text, in all of its richness, and I have been humbled to discover there is still so much to learn and appreciate about the Hebrew language. It is my hope that this handbook will instill both joy and humility in those who seek to extend our knowledge and appreciation of the Hebrew language.

I would like to thank my colleagues in the George W. Truett Theological Seminary at Baylor University. Their constant encouragement has sustained my work on the project. In particular, I would like to thank Dr. David Garland, Associate Dean for Academic Affairs, for his continued interest in, and investment in, my professional life. I am also grateful to the administration of Baylor University and the George W. Truett Theological Seminary for providing funds for a Summer Research Sabbatical, where some of the early work on this project was carried out.

There are several individuals that have provided assistance along the way. As my student assistant, Kyle Steinhauser spent considerable time tracking down articles and books for me in the early stages of this process, and has shown genuine interest in the project from the beginning. I would also like to thank Dr. Marty Culy, editor of the *Baylor Handbook on the Greek New Testament*. The New Testament series was already underway when Baylor University Press approached me about beginning a companion series on the Hebrew Bible. I have turned to Marty on numerous occasions to seek his advice, not only as editor of a series, but as a well-respected linguist. His insights have helped to sharpen the focus of this work in many ways. I would also like to thank Dr. Barry Bandstra, who read sections of this work, and offered constructive feedback on the project as a whole.

I am grateful to Baylor University Press for their support. Dr. Carey C. Newman, director of the Press, has provided much guidance through this project and the development of the series to which this volume belongs, *Baylor Handbook to the Hebrew Bible*. Appreciation also goes to Diane Smith, Production Editor, who has brought this project to its final form.

Finally, I would also like to thank my wife Tish and my three daughters, Hannah, Sarah, and Hope, for their unfailing support in my work, even when it required sacrifice on their part. My young daughters continue to remind me of the sheer joy found in reading Scripture. It is to them that I dedicate this work.

W. Dennis Tucker, Jr.

ABBREVIATIONS

AC	Bill Arnold and John H. Choi. *A Guide to Biblical Hebrew Syntax.* Cambridge: Cambridge University, 2003.
act	active
c	common
cop	copulative
constr	construct
f	feminine
GKC	Emil Kautzsch, ed. *Gesenius' Hebrew Grammar.* Translated and revised by A. E. Cowley. 2nd English edition. Oxford: Clarendon, 1910.
Hiph	Hiphil
Hith	Hithpael
impv	imperative
inf	infinitive
JM	Paul Joüon. *A Grammar of Biblical Hebrew.* Translated and revised by T. Muraoka. 2 vols. Subsidia Biblica 14. Rome: Pontifical Institute, 1993.
m	masculine
MNK	Christo H. J. van der Merwe, Jackie A. Naudé, and Jan H. Kroeze. *A Biblical Hebrew Reference Grammar. Biblical Languages: Hebrew* 3. Sheffield: Sheffield Academic. 1999.
Niph	Niphal
ptc	participle
part	particle
pl	plural
poss	possessive

pr   proper
prep   preposition
s   singular
WO   Bruce K. Waltke and Michael O'Connor. *An Introduction to Biblical Hebrew Syntax.* Winona Lake, Ind.: Eisenbrauns, 1990.

INTRODUCTION

The book of Jonah remains one of the first books often translated by beginning Hebrew students. The narrative format of the book coupled with the presumed familiarity of its story enable individuals with diverse Hebrew skills to make their first foray into the Hebrew Bible. Yet most beginning students still find the move from introductory grammar to biblical text to be a somewhat difficult transition. Issues of morphology give way to larger syntactic issues, at times leaving the student to struggle through a story that he or she first thought familiar. This handbook has been designed with that type of student in mind—one making the move from introductory grammar to biblical text. While there will no doubt be additional questions left unanswered for the reader, I have attempted to anticipate and address significant questions that might emerge as one moves through the Hebrew text of Jonah.

Although the treatment of Jonah that follows guides the reader through the Hebrew text, it remains distinct from most reference works currently available to students of the Hebrew Bible. A number of analytical keys now exist in print, with even more appearing on-line, thus making the need for another analytical key unnecessary. While this volume does provide the lexical forms for all verbs, it assumes that students with an introductory grasp of the Hebrew language can identify the remaining word classes (noun, preposition, conjunction, etc.). Unlike analytical keys, and other reference works, which provide only minimal guidance with syntactic issues, this volume places syntactic issues at the center of the discussion.

The series to which this volume belongs has been entitled the *Baylor Handbook on the Hebrew Bible*. The label "handbook" has been chosen carefully to reflect the scope and intent of the work. This handbook is not a commentary on Jonah and will not devote space to the type of theological and exegetical comments found in most commentaries, although at points, brief commentary on the text may be germane to the larger discussion. In addition, traditional introductory matters found in most treatments of biblical books such as authorship, provenance, and date are not considered. Readers interested in such matters should consult the commentaries and additional resources provided in the bibliography. As opposed to the multi-faceted aims of a commentary, this handbook remains singular in focus—to consider the Hebrew text and related issues, syntactic and otherwise. Similar to its sister series with Baylor University Press, *Baylor Handbook on the Greek New Testament*, this volume "serves as a 'prequel' to commentary proper. It primarily provides a guide to understanding the linguistic characteristics of the text from which the message of the text may then be derived" (Culy, xii).

The nature of the "handbook" format precludes significant interaction at every point with the secondary literature on the book of Jonah. Readers interested in the diverse interpretive strategies and subsequent theological commentary on specific texts should consult the secondary literature cited in the bibliography.

Methodological Issues

Introductory grammars tend to focus on individual word classes, with some attention to the structure of the Hebrew sentence itself. As a result, most beginning students come to a biblical text, such as Jonah, and simply continue with the same type of analysis. They look up each word and translate sentences. In the end, their translation closely resembles that of the analytical key they were using or their favorite modern translation. But more disturbing is the fact that students think such a rendering has demonstrated proficiency in reading and understanding the biblical text. In essence, students assume that micro-syntactic issues are their only concern in translation. And further, that strict attention to these matters will yield significant insights for interpretation. Students are frequently disappointed when such insights fail to appear from this type of analysis. This volume, however, attempts to move the students more towards thinking in a macro-syntactic way. Although there is much that can be done at the macro-syntactic level, the aim of this volume is modest—to focus attention on clauses and their syntactic function within the construction of a Hebrew text.

Many Biblical Hebrew grammarians have grown discontent with the traditional approaches to grammar and have turned to insights from modern linguistics in an attempt to generate newer models for studying Biblical Hebrew. The insights gained from modern linguistics have been indispensable in shifting the focus from micro-syntactic concerns to macro-syntactic concerns. Concern for the latter in no way negates the importance of the former; it merely extends the discussion in new and important ways.

This volume draws from the extensive work done in discourse analysis (also termed "text linguistics" or "discourse linguistics"). Although by no means the only approach to discourse analysis, the work of Robert Longacre and his approach to various "text-types" or "discourses" within the biblical text can be quite helpful in moving interpretation beyond merely identifying the constituent parts of a sentence. This approach begins by observing that within Biblical Hebrew texts a number of types or "discourses" can be identified. Each type has a particular function that is readily evident. Narrative discourse relates the events of a story (Gen 8). Predictive discourse speaks of an event in advance of its occurrence (I Sam 10:2-7). Hortatory discourse is meant to exhort someone to act in a particular manner (Job 2:9). Procedural discourse tells someone either how to do something or how something was done (Gen 27:1-4). And expository/descriptive discourse is meant to explain something or make a statement (2 Sam

12:7). (In his model, Longacre considers additional matters such as pre-peak, peak, post-peak episodes and closure. Such matters remain beyond the scope of the present volume.)

In addition to observing the function of each type of discourse, Longacre and others have observed that particular grammatical, and more specifically, verbal constructions are inherent to each discourse type. Further, within each type, a distinction can be made between mainline forms of communication, which serve as the "backbone" of the discourse, and off-the-line forms of communication, which serve as background or supportive material. Off-the-line material may also be the focus of the text—the narrator has shifted from the main sequence in order to draw attention to a particular topic. Although semantics may aid in distinguishing between mainline and off-the-line forms of communication, verbal constructions, as well as the structure of individual clauses, typically provides a more reliable guide. Within the book of Jonah, only three forms of discourse are present: narrative; hortatory; and expository. The discourse profile scheme of each is provided below. Although the terminology and structure follows that of Bryan Rocine's work on discourse analysis, and perhaps better reflects the nomenclature of many introductory grammars, it should be noted this his work is a derivative of Longacre's earlier work.

Narrative Discourse

Mainline:
  1a. *Wayyiqtol*
   1b. Pivotal/climactic event on the mainline: Isolated *weqatal*

Off-the-line:
   2. Topicalization: X + *qatal*
      3. Embedded direct speech
         4. Relative past background: *qatal* in dependent clause
         5. Relative non-past background: *yiqtol* in dependent clause

6. Backgrounded activities: Participle
7. Embedded procedural discourse
8. Transition marker: *wayyiqtol* of הָיָה
9. Scene setting: Verbless clause
10. Irrealis scene setting:
    Negation of any verb by לֹא

Similar to narrative texts in most languages, narrative discourse in Biblical Hebrew attempts to relate a story and the developing features of that story. The *wayyiqtol* (*waw* consecutive + imperfect) verb form serves as the "backbone" verbal form for moving the Hebrew narrative along, and occurs 84 times in the 48 verses of Jonah, clearly indicating the prominence of narrative discourse in the book. Additional "off-the-line" verbal forms appear in Jonah, performing a variety of functions in the presentation of the narrative. These off-the-line clauses and their function will be noted in the treatment of the text.

The hortatory discourse profile scheme includes the following elements:

Hortatory Discourse

Mainline: (All four are of equal value.)
  1a. Imperative
  1b. Jussive
  1c. Cohortative
  1d. *Weqatal* (for Mitigated Hortatory Discourse)

Off-the-line:
  2. Topicalization: X + Imperative (or Jussive or Cohortative)
  3. Prohibitive commands: אַל or לֹא + *yiqtol*
  4. Express possibility: *yiqtol*
  5. Consequence, purpose: *weqatal*
  6. Consequence, purpose: לֹא or פֶּן + *yiqtol*

   7. Consequence, purpose:
       Embedded predictive narrative
   8. Identification of problem:
       Embedded historical narrative
   9. Background activities: Participle
  10. Scene setting: Verbless clause

Hortatory discourse is the primary form of direct speech in the book of Jonah, with mainline forms occurring in the imperative (13 times), cohortative (2 times), and jussive (3 times). This form of direct speech is embedded (see below) throughout narrative discourse. Although in an off-the-line position, the *yiqtol* form occurs regularly throughout the sections of hortatory discourse, heightening the possibility of the desired outcomes.

Expository speech has a much smaller profile scheme. In his earlier work on the Joseph narrative, Longacre offered only tentative comments regarding expository discourse, noting in particular that "as the inverse of narrative discourse, expository discourse can be defined as discourse in which the most static verb forms of a language predominate" (1989, 111). The following profile scheme was developed by Rocine (see also Dawson, 116).

Expository Discourse

Mainline:
   1. Verbless Clause

Off-the-line:
   2. Clauses with *qatal* of הָיָה
     3. X + *qatal* of other roots
       4. Clauses with *yiqtol* with a present time reference
         5. *Qatal* and *yiqtol* in dependent clauses
           6. Embedded discourse

Expository discourse appears sporadically throughout Jonah as an embedded discourse (see below). The psalm in chapter 2, however, presents an extended example of expository discourse, with the psalm culminating in 2:10 (a verbless clause). The preceding clauses are understood as off-the-line clauses that build towards the final statement.

Embedded Discourse

The dominant discourse type in Jonah is narrative discourse. Chapters 1, 3, and 4 all exhibit significant characteristics of narrative, and chapter 2, which contains the lengthy psalm, begins and concludes with narrative (2:1-2, 11), thus enclosing the poem within the narrative structure of the book as a whole. Although narrative predominates throughout the book, direct speech does appear in the form of hortatory and expository discourses—direct speech which is embedded within the narrative flow of the text. For example, chapter 1 begins by signaling a narrative framework, but quickly shifts in verse 2 to an embedded hortatory discourse (the speech of Yahweh to Jonah). And then in verse 3, the text returns to narrative format. Thus the reader will find embedded discourse throughout the narrative portions of Jonah, and even in the poetic section, where oral narrative discourse is embedded within an expository discourse. The shift from one discourse to another is evident by the appearance of "discourse switch cues." The most frequently occurring discourse switch cue is the verb אָמַר which moves the narrative discourse to some form of direct speech, usually hortatory discourse. One should note, however, that every occurrence of אָמַר should not be construed as a discourse switch cue (cf. 2:11). The use of אָמַר and other discourse switch cues are indicated throughout the treatment of Jonah.

Syntactic Labels

When speaking of Hebrew nouns, a number of Hebrew grammars continue to use nomenclature that is more at home in Latin and Greek. In those languages, grammatical relationships are expressed by declensions. Similarly, Hebrew nouns are frequently identified as "nominative," "genitive," "dative," or "accusative," despite the fact that there is nothing inherent in the form of the noun itself that can aid in that determination. As opposed to the Greek word λογου, which can be identified as a genitive masculine singular noun, the precise "case" for the Hebrew word דָּבָר cannot so easily be identified in isolation. In fact, the "case" for Hebrew nouns can only be determined at the syntactic level. In other words, what makes a noun an "accusative" is its function in the clause or sentence, not the grammatical construction of the word itself.

In their reference grammar, van der Merwe, Naudé, and Kroeze acknowledge that case endings are not present in Biblical Hebrew and resort to other terminology in an effort to better reflect the characteristics of the language itself. Particularly helpful are their designations "adjuncts" and "complements." At the syntactic level, adjuncts are non-verbal elements that can be removed from the predicate, or verbal phrase, without disrupting or influencing the construction. Adverbs, prepositional phrases, and some noun phrases function as an adjunct to the main verb. Frequently in Jonah, prepositional phrases function in this capacity.

At the syntactic level, complements are obligatory, non-omissible, and non-verbal parts of the predicate or verb phrase. Unlike the adjunct, if a complement is removed, the construction is altered. Complements are usually nouns or prepositional phrases that are added to or combined with verbs. Often these nouns or prepositional phrases indicate the direct or indirect object of the verb. Rather than assigning "cases" to nouns and prepositional phrases throughout Jonah, I have opted to follow van der Merwe, Naudé, and Kroeze, and in so doing, I have indicated whether non-verbal material is an adjunct or complement to the verb. In places where the noun is the direct object of the verb and does not appear in a prepositional phrase, the noun is simply titled "direct object."

In attempting to describe the function of prepositions, I occasionally revert to case language, but only in an effort to describe the semantic contribution of a preposition. Hence, a preposition might be described as functioning in a "locative sense," but that in no way concedes that the object of the preposition is locative in form, only that together they generate a sense nearer to what is understood as a locative in other languages.

Format of Handbook

A brief word on the format of the handbook is in order. The handbook has been designed for the reader already working with a full Hebrew text of Jonah at hand. To assist in the study of the text, a translation of the Hebrew text has been provided at the beginning of each section or pericope in an effort to aid readers in seeing how the various clauses and sentences function together in the larger text. The full Hebrew text is provided in a verse by verse format, and is justified on the right margin. In an effort to highlight the function of clauses and their relationship with one another, clauses appear beneath the full Hebrew verse, and they are justified on the left margin. Immediately following each clause is an analysis of that clause as a whole, with comments related to the function of the clause, its discourse type, and related syntactic matters. Beneath each clause, and indented, the individual words or groups of words that comprise that clause are discussed in detail. Where there is only one word in the clause (i.e., 1:12, שָׂאוּנִי), the identification of that word and related comments are included in the analysis of the clause itself. A glossary appears at the end of the book, providing students with basic definitions to words employed throughout the book.

A HANDBOOK ON THE HEBREW TEXT OF JONAH

Jonah 1:1-3

¹Now the word of the LORD came to Jonah, son of Amittai: ²"Go immediately to Nineveh, the great city, and call against her for their wickedness has come up before me." ³But Jonah set out in order to flee to Tarshish away from the presence of God. He went down to Joppa and chanced upon a ship coming from Tarshish. He paid its fare and went down in it in order to go with them towards Tarshish, away from the presence of the Lord.

1:1　וַיְהִי֙ דְּבַר־יְהוָ֔ה אֶל־יוֹנָ֥ה בֶן־אֲמִתַּ֖י לֵאמֹֽר׃

Narrative discourse—mainline. The presence of the *wayyiqtol* form indicates that the narrative opens on the mainline. וַיְהִי is best understood as a discourse marker, signaling the beginning of a narrative that presumably follows a preceding event or scene. Or to put it differently, the verb signals that "it is therefore part of the mainstream of a greater narration" (MNK, 331–32). The obvious problem is that it stands at the beginning of the book—with no preceding event clearly in view. Perhaps the narrator's deviation from normal Hebrew construction and unexpected use of conventional language at the beginning of the book suggests the unconventional nature of the remainder of the book (Trible, 1994, 125).

וַיְהִי. Qal *wayyiqtol* 3 m s from הָיָה. When וַיְהִי appears elsewhere, an impersonal subject is often understood, rendering the phrase, "and *it* came to pass," or "and then *it* was" (Gen 4:3; Ex 19:16; Esth 1:1), yet in these instances rarely is there a noun provided to serve as subject of the verb. In Jonah 1:1, however, the subsequent noun, דְּבַר־יְהוָה, operates as the subject, thus rendering the phrase, "Now the word of the LORD came. . . ." Sasson attempts to render the verb temporally, "When the LORD's command . . . was" (67), but such a rendering makes the transition to the main clause in the next verse awkward.

Kamp suggests that the transition marker וַיְהִי actually serves to divide the text of Jonah into five episodes or narratives (1:1-4a; 1:4b-2:1a; 2:1b-11b; 3:1a–4:7c; 4:8a-11c). See Kamp, 89–91.

דְּבַר־יְהוָה. The construct phrase indicates a relationship of possession (MNK, 198). Other grammars refer to this as a "possessive genitive." The verb + subject phrase (וַיְהִי דְּבַר־יְהוָה) + אֶל "is found only when contexts and circumstances regarding the prophet and his mission are already established" (Sasson, 67), as often seen in the Elijah narratives.

אֶל־יוֹנָה. The prepositional phrase serves as a complement to the verb, with the preposition marking the indirect object.

בֶן־אֲמִתַּי. The construct phrase stands in apposition to יוֹנָה. The absolute noun in the construct phrase functions attributively. On the role and frequency of the appositional phrase in Hebrew, see WO 226–34 (see AC, 21–24; JM, 477–81).

לֵאמֹר. Prep + Qal inf constr. The infinitive form of אָמַר is best understood as having "become grammaticalized as a complementizer" (Miller, 206). The absence of typical features associated with an infinitive, particularly the governing of objects, adverbial phrases or prepositional phrases, suggests that it has retained a different function, namely that of a complementizer. Miller explains that "a complementizer precedes its complement without intervening constituents" (207). In the present sentence, לֵאמֹר appears at the end of the quotative frame (initial clause) and introduces the complement, i.e., the quotation of direct speech. In addition to functioning as a complementizer, לֵאמֹר also functions as a discourse switch cue, noting the shift from narrative discourse to hortatory discourse.

1:2   ק֠וּם לֵ֧ךְ אֶל־נִֽינְוֵ֛ה הָעִ֥יר הַגְּדוֹלָ֖ה וּקְרָ֣א עָלֶ֑יהָ כִּֽי־
עָלְתָ֥ה רָעָתָ֖ם לְפָנָֽי:

קוּם לֵ֧ךְ אֶל־נִֽינְוֵה הָעִיר הַגְּדוֹלָה. Embedded hortatory discourse—mainline. Imperatives are mainline verb forms in hortatory discourse. In general, hortatory discourse is meant to persuade the audience or alter the behavior of the audience (Rocine, 107; Dawson, 99).

קוּם לֵךְ. Qal impv 2 m s – Qal impv 2 m s from הָלַךְ. In an asyndetic construction of this sort, the principle idea is introduced in the second verb, with the first having a functional, rather than, semantic value. In such constructions, Andersen has suggested that the first imperative functions as a hortatory particle, thus denoting that the clause is an exclamation (57). Waltke and O'Connor follow similarly, suggesting that the imperative may function as a type of interjection (574). Both the JPS and the NRSV attempt to convey the nature of such a construction with "Go at once." Both verbs, in similar constructions, appear frequently in prophetic commissioning formulas (cf. I Kgs 17:9; Jer 13:4-6; Ezek 3:22).

אֶל־נִֽינְוֵה. The preposition functions in a terminative sense marking movement towards something or some place (AC, 97).

הָעִיר הַגְּדוֹלָה. Because a name cannot be modified directly by an adjective, הָעִיר is inserted (WO, 258), creating an attribute in apposition (JM, 513). Attributive use of adjective.

וּקְרָא עָלֶיהָ. Embedded hortatory discourse—mainline. The use of the imperative maintains the discourse at the mainline level.

וּקְרָא. Waw cop + Qal impv 2 m s. In the present construction, the two imperatives (קוּם לֵךְ) are linked to the third imperative (קְרָא)

by means of a *waw* copulative. The *waw* has no additional semantic value beyond simply linking imperatives with the same addressee.

עָלֶיהָ. Oppositional sense of the preposition. Objective pronoun. A similar phrase appears in 3:2 with the notable exception of a different preposition—וּקְרָא אֵלֶיהָ. Sasson has argued that the use of עַל in 1:2 presents a more foreboding nuance, "imposing an (unpleasant) fate upon something" (75). Others have made similar observations in attempting to establish an intended difference between עַל and אֶל (Landes, 158).

כִּי־עָלְתָה רָעָתָם לְפָנָי. Embedded hortatory discourse—off-the-line. The particle כִּי indicates that the clause itself is a subordinate clause, yet more critically, the subordinate particle כִּי can also signal the presence an embedded discourse. Embedded within the larger hortatory discourse is a brief narrative discourse.

כִּי־עָלְתָה. Particle + Qal *qatal* 3 f s from עָלָה. A *qatal* within a dependent clause indicates events that are background to the main-line of the discourse. In Jonah, whenever *qatal* verbs appear in clauses initiated by a particle (כִּי, אֲשֶׁר) and those clauses report happenings, such events are considered "demoted" happenings. They are "grammatically marginalized in reference to the main clauses or are attributive to a noun head" (Longacre and Hwang, 347).

רָעָתָם. Subject of עָלָה. Earlier, feminine singular pronouns have been employed when speaking of the city proper, but here the shift to the masculine plural form is probably best understood metonymically—representing the individuals within Nineveh. In chapter 3, Nineveh as a city is mentioned (v 3), but when the actions of its inhabitants are specified, the narrator shifts to masculine plural language (v 5). Sasson notes the remote possibility that the final *mem* could be understood as an enclitic, hence rendering the phrase "her (Nineveh's) wickedness" (75).

לְפָנָי. The preposition is understood locationally, with the prepositional phrase functioning as an adjunct to the verb. Objective pronoun.

1.3 וַיָּקָם יוֹנָה לִבְרֹחַ תַּרְשִׁישָׁה מִלִּפְנֵי יְהוָה וַיֵּרֶד יָפוֹ
וַיִּמְצָא אָנִיָּה ׀ בָּאָה תַרְשִׁישׁ וַיִּתֵּן שְׂכָרָהּ וַיֵּרֶד בָּהּ
לָבוֹא עִמָּהֶם תַּרְשִׁישָׁה מִלִּפְנֵי יְהוָה׃

וַיָּקָם יוֹנָה. Narrative discourse—mainline. Although the final clause in verse 2 constituted a narrative embedded within the larger hortatory discourse, the first clause in verse 3 contains a *wayyiqtol*, which serves as a discourse switch cue, alerting the reader to the shift from hortatory to narrative discourse.

וַיָּקָם. Qal *wayyiqtol* 3 m s from קוּם. Although the verb form is a *wayyiqtol*, suggesting a progression in the narrative, the verb may be better understood as standing in contrast to what has previously been stated. Thus rather than translating the *wayyiqtol* as "and then," the *wayyiqtol* might translated better as a disjunctive, "but" (see Trible, 1994, 128).

יוֹנָה. Subject of יָקָם.

לִבְרֹחַ תַּרְשִׁישָׁה מִלִּפְנֵי יְהוָה. Narrative discourse—mainline. The infinitive + לְ introduces a subordinate purpose clause.

לִבְרֹחַ. Prep + Qal inf constr.

תַּרְשִׁישָׁה. Pronoun + locative *he*.

מִלִּפְנֵי יְהוָה. The preposition indicates spatial positioning, denoting movement away from an object. The construct phrase expresses a relationship of possession (see 1:1, דְּבַר־יְהוָה).

וַיֵּרֶד יָפוֹ. Narrative discourse—mainline. The *wayyiqtol* verb form continues the narrative discourse.

וַיֵּרֶד. Qal *wayyiqtol* 3 m s from יָרַד. The term is repeated in 1:3, 1:5, and 2:7, operating as a metaphor for Jonah's action of fleeing.

יָפוֹ. Verbal complement. With verbs of motion, nouns that are non-objects (not the direct object of the verb) are considered complements (MNK, 244).

וַיִּמְצָא אֳנִיָּה. Narrative discourse—mainline.

וַיִּמְצָא. Qal *wayyiqtol* 3 m s. In addition to the primary meaning of "to find," מָצָא carries a more nuanced meaning that appears better suited to its usage here. The term can mean "to meet by chance" or "to come upon unexpectedly" (BDB, 593).

אֳנִיָּה. Dir obj of מָצָא. The feminine forms of substantives may be used to indicate an individual component belonging to a class which is denoted by the masculine form (GKC, 394). In this case, אֳנִי (masculine) meaning "fleet of ships" is the larger class from which (אֳנִיָּה) is derived.

בָּאָה תַרְשִׁישׁ. Narrative discourse—off-the-line. Within narrative discourse, a participle is used to provide background information.

בָּאָה. Qal act ptc f s. Attributive participle modifying אֳנִיָּה. The verb would be Qal *qatal* 3 f s were the accent on the first syllable, but its placement on the final syllable indicates its function here as a participle. Many translators have assumed this participle to be a "future predicate participle" (AC, 81), also known as a *futurum instans*. As a result, translators have assumed this implies the ship is "about to go to Tarshish," or more simply put, the NIV's translation: "a ship *bound* for that port" (see GKC 356; Snaith, 10). One should note, however, that the particle הִנֵּה often appears when indicating impending action (cf. Gen 6:17; Deut 31:16). Sasson has challenged the traditional reading as well, suggesting that בּוֹא typically directs the movement towards the narrator in the story, while הָלַךְ is reserved for motion away from the narrator (Sasson, 82). The fact that תַרְשִׁישׁ lacks the *he* directive, despite its use on the same term both before and after, may lend further credence to Sasson's suggestion. In this instance, the term may imply the ship has returned from תַרְשִׁישׁ.

תַּרְשִׁישׁ. Pr noun. Verbal complement. See discussion on יָפוֹ above.

וַיִּתֵּן שְׂכָרָהּ. Narrative discourse—mainline. The appearance of a *wayyiqtol* returns the narrative to the mainline of verbal action.

וַיִּתֵּן. Qal *wayyiqtol* 3 m s from נָתַן.

שְׂכָרָהּ. Dir obj. Possessive pronoun. The pronominal suffix should be understood as anaphoric, referring back to אֳנִיָּה, yet often the term is translated with reference to Jonah. The LXX adjusts the text to read και εδωκη το ναυλον αυτου ("and he paid *his* fare"). Modern translations have either ignored the suffix (NIV, NASB: "paid the fare") or they have modified it to read masculine (NRSV, "paid his fare"). The feminine suffix should be retained as it makes sense given a proper reading of שָׂכַר. Throughout the Hebrew Bible, שָׂכַר refers to the wages one is paid for service or work (cf. Deut 24:15). The noun + feminine suffix suggests that Jonah paid "her (the ship's) wages." Arguably, Jonah hired the ship and its crew to sail him to Tarshish (Sasson, 83–84).

וַיֵּרֶד בָּהּ. Narrative discourse—mainline.

וַיֵּרֶד. Qal *wayyiqtol* 3 m s from יָרַד.

בָּהּ. The preposition is understood locationally, with the prepositional phrase functioning as an adjunct to the verb. Objective pronoun.

לָבוֹא עִמָּהֶם תַּרְשִׁישָׁה מִלִּפְנֵי יְהוָה. Narrative discourse—mainline. Although the clause is properly understood as a purpose clause, its function is to modify the main clause, not move the discourse to an "off-the-line" construction.

לָבוֹא. Prep + Qal inf constr. The infinitive introduces a subordinate clause, best understood as a purpose clause—"in order to . . ." (WO, 606–7).

עִמָּהֶם. The pronominal suffix should be read as cataphoric, pointing towards the sailors mentioned in 1:4. The preposition עִם implies accompaniment (WO, 219). Sasson suggests that the idiom לָבוֹא עִם

is meant to suggest that Jonah has become a member of the crew (Sasson, 84). Whether such a reading can be ascertained from the text is questionable, but clearly the phrase intends to associate Jonah with the sailors.

תַּרְשִׁישָׁה. Pr noun + locative *he*.

מִלִּפְנֵי יְהוָה. See above.

Jonah 1:4-6

[4]But the LORD hurled a great wind into the sea and a strong tempest came upon the sea and the ship thought it would break up. [5]Then the sailors were afraid and each cried out to his god. They hurled the vessels which were on the ship into the sea in order to make it lighter for them. In the meantime, Jonah had gone down into the recesses of the ship and had lain down and fallen asleep. [6]Then the captain of the sailors came to him and said, "What are you doing asleep? Rise up and call to your god. Perhaps that god will give thought to us so that we may not perish."

1:4   וַיהוָה הֵטִיל רוּחַ־גְּדוֹלָה אֶל־הַיָּם וַיְהִי סַעַר־גָּדוֹל
בַּיָּם וְהָאֳנִיָּה חִשְּׁבָה לְהִשָּׁבֵר

וַיהוָה הֵטִיל רוּחַ־גְּדוֹלָה אֶל־הַיָּם. Narrative discourse—off-the-line. The X + *qatal* construction has a focus-shifting function called "topicalization." Such a construction is used to clarify a switch in the participants of the story, or introduce a new participant into the story (Rocine, 23).

וַיהוָה. A *waw* before a non-verb constituent has a disjunctive role.

הֵטִיל. Hiph *qatal* 3 m s from טוּל. The four-fold use of טוּל in chapter 1 could be understood as a form of diaphora.

רוּחַ־גְּדוֹלָה. Direct object of טוּל. Attributive use of adjective.

אֶל־הַיָּם. The preposition אֶל is used in a terminative sense, hence, "into."

וַיְהִי סַעַר־גָּדוֹל בַּיָּם. Narrative discourse—mainline. Although וַיְהִי often serves as a transition marker, it may also function as an ordinary verb, meant to be treated on par with the mainline events of the narrative (MNK, 333).

וַיְהִי. Qal *wayyiqtol* 3 m s from הָיָה. Grammatically, there are two possible subjects for the verb. The verb could be understood as having an impersonal subject, or סַעַר could operate as the subject.

סַעַר־גָּדוֹל. Subj of וַיְהִי. Attributive use of adjective.

בַּיָּם. The preposition בְּ indicates spatial localization—the so-called *beth locale*.

וְהָאֳנִיָּה חִשְּׁבָה לְהִשָּׁבֵר. Narrative discourse—off-the-line. On the focus-shifting feature of the X + *qatal* construction, see above. As before, the construction fronts a new participant in the story.

וְהָאֳנִיָּה. Subj of חָשַׁב. Although אֳנִיָּה appeared previously in verse 3 as a direct object, the structure of the clause gives new prominence to the noun.

חִשְּׁבָה. Piel *qatal* 3 f s from חָשַׁב. The attribution of human activity ("thinking") to an inanimate object is an example of prosopopoeia.

לְהִשָּׁבֵר. Prep + Niph inf constr. The infinitive construct serves as a verbal complement to חָשַׁב (WO, 606). The pairing of a transitive verb with a Niphal intransitive verb often results in a middle voice (WO, 381). In the middle voice, the agent is both subject and object of the action.

The phrase חִשְּׁבָה לְהִשָּׁבֵר operates onomatopoeically, attempting to capture "the sound of the planks cracking when tortured by raging waters" (Sasson, 97). Further, assonance links these two words

together emphasizing both the sound and significance of the event
(Trible, 1994, 132).

1:5 וַיִּֽירְא֣וּ הַמַּלָּחִ֗ים וַֽיִּזְעֲקוּ֮ אִ֣ישׁ אֶל־אֱלֹהָיו֒ וַיָּטִ֨לוּ
אֶת־הַכֵּלִ֜ים אֲשֶׁ֤ר בָּֽאֳנִיָּה֙ אֶל־הַיָּ֔ם לְהָקֵ֖ל מֵֽעֲלֵיהֶ֑ם
וְיוֹנָ֗ה יָרַד֙ אֶל־יַרְכְּתֵ֣י הַסְּפִינָ֔ה וַיִּשְׁכַּ֖ב וַיֵּרָדַֽם׃

וַיִּֽירְא֣וּ הַמַּלָּחִים. Narrative discourse—mainline.

וַיִּֽירְאוּ. Qal *wayyiqtol* 3 m p from יָרֵא. יָרֵא is a stative verb that
is used both transitively and intransitively in Jonah. Here in verse 5,
the verb appears as an intransitive, but in verse 9 the obverse is the
case. Note also that verse 5 contains six independent clauses. The first
three clauses pertaining to the activity of the sailors are juxtaposed
with three subsequent clauses pertaining to the activity (or inactivity)
of Jonah. Earlier in the story Jonah appears to be identified with the
sailors (v 3), but through the structure of the independent clauses in
verse 5, Jonah now appears in stark contrast to them.

הַמַּלָּחִים. Subject of וַיִּֽירְאוּ.

וַֽיִּזְעֲקוּ אִישׁ אֶל־אֱלֹהָיו. Narrative discourse—mainline.

וַֽיִּזְעֲקוּ. Qal *wayyiqtol* 3 m p. The idiom אֶל + זָעַק denotes calling
out to someone (particularly a deity) or something for help.

אִישׁ. אִישׁ is a substantive operating as a collective noun (see GKC,
395). Typically a singular collective noun functions as the subject of a
verb in plural form (see Judg 15:10). Joüon suggests that the collective
noun itself can be identified through its connection with an adjective,
pronoun, or a verb that appears in the plural (497 n. 1).

אֶל־אֱלֹהָיו. The prepositional phrase functions as a complement
to the verb, marking out the goal of the saying process (MNK, 278).
Traditional grammarians refer to this as the simple dative use of the
preposition (WO, 193). Possessive pronoun.

וַיָּטִלוּ אֶת־הַכֵּלִים. Narrative discourse—mainline.

וַיָּטִלוּ. Hiph *wayyiqtol* 3 m p from טוּל.

אֶת־הַכֵּלִים. Dir obj of וַיָּטִלוּ.

אֲשֶׁר בָּאֳנִיָּה. Narrative discourse—off-the-line. The relative pronoun אֲשֶׁר introduces a subordinate clause meant to modify הַכֵּלִים. Subordinate clauses are considered off-the-line because they typically provide background information to the main narrative.

אֲשֶׁר. Rel pronoun. Introduces a subordinate clause in which the antecedent הַכֵּלִים serves as the subject of a verbless clause.

בָּאֳנִיָּה. The preposition בְּ indicates spatial localization—the so-called *beth locale*.

אֶל־הַיָּם. Defective clause. The clause is defective because its connection with the clause וַיָּטִלוּ אֶת־הַכֵּלִים has been interrupted by the subordinate clause אֲשֶׁר בָּאֳנִיָּה. The prepositional phrase is intended as a adjunct to the verb וַיָּטִלוּ. Terminative use of the preposition.

לְהָקֵל מֵעֲלֵיהֶם. Narrative discourse—mainline. The infinitive construct with a לְ indicates a subordinate purpose clause meant to explain the statements in the mainline clause (וַיָּטִלוּ . . .).

לְהָקֵל. Prep + Hiph inf constr. The verbal root is a geminate (קָלַל).

מֵעֲלֵיהֶם. The prepositional phrase stands as an adjunct to the infinitive with a locative sense. Objective pronoun.

וְיוֹנָה יָרַד אֶל־יַרְכְּתֵי הַסְּפִינָה. Narrative discourse—off-the-line. The *waw* + X + *qatal* construction moves the narrative off the mainline by shifting the focus to the fronted subject of the clause, יוֹנָה, thus shifting the focus from that of the sailors to that of Jonah.

וְיוֹנָה. Whereas the word order in all three clauses concerning the activity of the sailors is unmarked, the word order in the first clause concerning Jonah is marked, thus highlighting Jonah.

יָרַד. Qal *qatal* 3 m s. A fronted subject in a clause may signal an anterior construction (for an extended treatment of the anterior construction, see Ziony Zevit). Van der Merwe, Naudé, and Kroeze contend, "This construction refers to events that happened, relative to a temporal sequence of events, 'in the meanwhile'" (349). Thus while most translations capture this break in sequencing with the use of a pluperfect, "had gone down," such a rendering fails to suggest the near simultaneity of events, and hence looses the effect of the comparison between the activity of the sailors and the inactivity of Jonah. Allen attempts to observe this nuance with his translation, "Meanwhile Jonah had gone down . . ." (206).

אֶל־יַרְכְּתֵי הַסְּפִינָה. The preposition אֶל is used in a terminative sense (see 1:4). יַרְכְּתֵי is the dual form of the feminine noun יָרֵךְ, which can mean "base" or "side." In the dual, however, the term can connote "extreme parts," or "recesses" (BDB 438). The term is employed elsewhere when speaking of Sheol (Is 14:15; Ezek 32:23)—serving to link the movement in chapter 1 with the experience articulated in chapter 2.

When speaking of the ship previously, אֳנִיָּה has been employed, but in verse 5, the terminology shifts to הַסְּפִינָה. Although the term is a *hapax legomenon,* the root ספן ("to cover") is often cited in discussions (Domeris, 281–82; Allen, 207 n. 24; Sasson, 101). Despite the obscurity of the term, its appearance is evidence of the narrator's penchant for synonyms throughout the text.

וַיִּשְׁכַּב. Narrative discourse—mainline. The *wayyiqtol* returns the narrative to the mainline, continuing the movement of the narrative. Qal *wayyiqtol* 3 m s.

וַיֵּרָדַם. Narrative discourse—mainline. Qal *wayyiqtol* 3 m s. The verb occurs only 11 times in the Hebrew Bible (twice in Jonah), often referring to a deep sleep. Perhaps humorously, the translators of the LXX inserted the phrase και ειρρεγχεν suggesting that not only was Jonah in a deep sleep, but he was snoring! As Magonet has noted, in the Hebrew Bible the verb has two distinct meanings: 1) a sleep associated with revelation (Job 4:13; 33:15; Dan 8:18); 2) a deep sleep associated with being close to death (Judg 4:21; Ps 76:7). Since revelation does not seem within the purview of the narrative, Magonet suggests this is the first hint at Jonah's "death wish" (68). Although there are other words to convey sleep in Hebrew (יָשֵׁן), the choice of רדם appears intentional in suggesting the full extent of Jonah's movement (or lack thereof)—"going down," "lying down," "sleeping"—in response to the storm. Note also in the structure of verse 5, the movement of the sailors begins with simple clauses and builds to a longer clause suggesting great activity. The three clauses devoted to Jonah suggest just the opposite—a longer clause suggesting activity, culminating with two shorter clauses suggesting inactivity.

1:6   וַיִּקְרַב אֵלָיו רַב הַחֹבֵל וַיֹּאמֶר לוֹ מַה־לְּךָ נִרְדָּם קוּם
קְרָא אֶל־אֱלֹהֶיךָ אוּלַי יִתְעַשֵּׁת הָאֱלֹהִים לָנוּ וְלֹא
נֹאבֵד:

וַיִּקְרַב אֵלָיו רַב הַחֹבֵל. Narrative discourse—mainline.

וַיִּקְרַב. Qal wayyiqtol 3 m s.

אֵלָיו. The preposition אֶל is terminative, marking the goal of some type of movement. The order of the clause (V + PP + S) is not marked. Words such as אֵלָיו have a deitic function and necessarily stand as close to the verb as possible (on an exception to this rule, see MNK, 341).

רַב הַחֹבֵל. Subject of קָרַב. הַחֹבֵל is understood as a collective word for the sailors (Wolff, 113). The term is used similarly in Ezekiel 27:8, 27-29, again demonstrating the narrator's penchant for synonyms.

וַיֹּאמֶר לוֹ. Narrative discourse—mainline.

וַיֹּאמֶר. Qal *wayyiqtol* 3 m s. The *wayyiqtol* form of אָמַר serves as a discourse switch cue, signaling the transition from one form of discourse (narrative) to another (hortatory discourse).

לוֹ. The prepositional phrase functions as a complement to the verb, marking out the indirect object. Objective pronoun.

מַה־לְּךָ נִרְדָּם. Embedded hortatory discourse—off-the-line. In hortatory discourse, participial clauses indicate backgrounded activities. Prior to the imperative that is to follow, the רַב הַחֹבֵל makes reference to the activity of Jonah.

מַה־לְּךָ. The inanimate pronoun מַה is coupled with a *lamed* of interest (a "lamed of interest" marks the object for or against whom the action is intended). In such a construction, "the question concerns the object of *l* in a loosely or elliptically defined way" (WO, 323). Objective pronoun.

נִרְדָּם. Niph ptc m s. Although the participle can be translated as a vocative, Joüon notes that the definite article is frequently attached when reference is made to persons who are present (509). The participle functions as a predicate adjective.

קוּם קְרָא אֶל־אֱלֹהֶיךָ. Embedded hortatory discourse—mainline. The imperative is the mainline verb form for hortatory discourse.

קוּם קְרָא. Qal impv 2 m s – Qal impv 2 m s. These are the first words spoken by a human in the book and like the first words spoken by Yahweh (v 2), they appear in an asyndetic construction. As noted in verse 2, in an asyndetic construction of this sort, the principle idea is introduced in the second verb, with the first having a functional, rather than, semantic value. The first imperative may function as a hortatory participle, denoting the exclamatory nature of the clause. The first imperative may also be functioning as a *double entendre*. While it may have a unique function within the asyndetic construction, the verb קוּם also appears to stand in contrast to the two verbs describing the reclining state of Jonah, וַיִּשְׁכַּב and וַיֵּרָדַם.

אֶל־אֱלֹהֶיךָ. The prepositional phrase functions as a complement to the verb, marking out the goal of the saying process. Possessive pronoun.

אוּלַי יִתְעַשֵּׁת הָאֱלֹהִים לָנוּ. Embedded hortatory discourse—off-the-line. A *yiqtol* in hortatory discourse may express possibility.

אוּלַי. Modal adv. Unlike other adverbs, modal adverbs relate to an entire clause, accentuating the probability or possibility of the events to which a clause refers. The presence of a modal adverb only heightens the notion of possibility indicated by the presence of a *yiqtol* in hortatory discourse.

יִתְעַשֵּׁת. Hith *yiqtol* 3 m s from עָשַׁת. An Aramaism that appears only here in the Hebrew Bible (the root occurs also in the Aramaic portion of Daniel [6:4]).

הָאֱלֹהִים. Subject of יִתְעַשֵּׁת. The definite article here should probably be construed as a demonstrative pronoun (GKC, 404; Allen 206, n. 16).

לָנוּ. The prepositional phrase is a complement to the verb, with the preposition marking out the indirect object.

וְלֹא נֹאבֵד. Embedded hortatory discourse—off-the-line. *Waw* cop + neg – Qal *yiqtol* 1 c p. Within hortatory discourse, a לֹא + *yiqtol* construction moves the discourse off the mainline, indicating a consequence or purpose statement. The *waw* copulative functions as a subordinating conjunction, indicating the result of the content from the preceding clause (MNK, 299). Rather than translating the *waw* as the simple conjunction "and," the *waw* is better translated as "in order that" or "so that."

Jonah 1:7-12

[7]And then they said, one to another, "Come, let us cast lots so that we may know on whose account this disaster has come upon us."

Then they cast lots and the lot fell to Jonah. ⁸Then they said to him, "Tell us on whose account has this disaster come upon us? What is your task and from where do you come? What is your country and from which nationality are you?" ⁹And then he said to them, "I am a Hebrew and I fear the LORD God of the heavens —the one who made the sea and the dry land." ¹⁰Then the men were greatly afraid and they said to him, "What is this you have done" (for the men knew that he was fleeing from the presence of the LORD because he had told them). ¹¹Then they said to him, "What shall we do to you in order that the sea might quiet down around us for the sea is growing stormier?" ¹²And he said to them, "Pick me up and hurl me into the sea so that the sea around you might quiet down because I admit that it is on my account that this great tempest has come upon you."

1:7 וַיֹּאמְר֞וּ אִ֣ישׁ אֶל־רֵעֵ֗הוּ לְכוּ֙ וְנַפִּ֣ילָה גֽוֹרָל֔וֹת וְנֵ֣דְעָ֔ה בְּשֶׁלְּמִ֛י הָרָעָ֥ה הַזֹּ֖את לָ֑נוּ וַיַּפִּ֙לוּ֙ גּֽוֹרָל֔וֹת וַיִּפֹּ֥ל הַגּוֹרָ֖ל עַל־יוֹנָֽה:

וַיֹּאמְרוּ אִישׁ אֶל־רֵעֵהוּ. Narrative discourse—mainline.

וַיֹּאמְרוּ. Qal *wayyiqtol* 3 m p. The verb functions as a discourse switch cue. On the function of אָמַר in introducing the content of a speech event, see Miller (386–93).

אִישׁ אֶל־רֵעֵהוּ. This construction appears frequently in the Hebrew Bible, indicating a reciprocal phrase (BDB, 946). On the use of אִישׁ with a plural verb, see 1:5.

לְכוּ. Embedded hortatory discourse—mainline. The verb אָמַר in the previous clause indicates a discourse switch to direct speech. The presence of an imperative signals a move to hortatory discourse. Qal impv 2 m s from הָלַךְ. See below on the implications of the imperative followed by another volitive verb form.

וְנַפִּילָה גּוֹרָלוֹת. Embedded hortatory discourse—mainline. In addition to imperatives, jussive and cohortative verbs constitute the mainline of hortatory discourse.

וְנַפִּילָה. *Waw* cop + Hiphil *yiqtol* 1 c p + coh *he*. In an impv + *waw* + cohortative construction (where the imperative is either קוּם or הְלֵךְ), the initial imperative serves as an exhortation to execute the following directive (MNK, 172). In such a construction, the *waw* is rarely translated (cf. NRSV, JPS). The use of גּוֹרָל with נָפַל has a technical or idiomatic usage (Harman, 129), and depending on the events being conveyed, may necessitate a different verbal stem. The Qal form of נָפַל is employed when speaking of the lot "falling," but when the text speaks of "casting" lots, the Hiphil form is required.

גּוֹרָלוֹת. M p noun. Direct object of נָפַל. גּוֹרָלוֹת may be classified as an irregular noun since it is masculine in gender, but takes the feminine ending in the plural.

וְנֵדְעָה. Embedded hortatory discourse—mainline. *Waw* cop + Qal *yiqtol* 1 c p + coh *he*. After a cohortative, the *waw* + cohortative generates a purpose clause in which the waw is quite often translated as "so that" (MNK, 171).

בְּשֶׁלְמִי הָרָעָה הַזֹּאת לָנוּ. Embedded hortatory discourse—off-the-line. The verbless clause provides background or explanatory information in hortatory discourse—momentarily shifting the intent of the discourse from altering behavior to identifying information necessary for understanding the scene.

בְּשֶׁלְמִי. Prep + rel part + prep + inter. The compound introduces a verbless clause that serves as a complement to the verb יָדַע (traditionally, such a clause has been understood as a substantival clause with an accusative function [see AC, 171–73]).

הָרָעָה. הָרָעָה serves as the predicate of the verbless clause. The semantic domain of רָעָה is vast, and the author of Jonah weaves the word throughout the narrative, forcing the context to determine the precise nuance of the term in each case. Although רָעָה appears in 1:2 apparently meaning "evil," or "wickedness," that does not seem to be the case in its present context.

הַזֹּאת. Attributive use of demonstrative pronoun, modifying הָרָעָה.

לָנוּ. The preposition is understood locationally, with the prepositional phrase functioning as an adjunct to the verb.

וַיַּפִּלוּ גּוֹרָלוֹת. Narrative discourse—mainline. The *wayyiqtol* verb form serves as a discourse switch cue, indicating that the discourse has shifted from direct speech (hortatory) back to narrative.

וַיַּפִּלוּ. Hiph *wayyiqtol* 3 m p from נָפַל.

גּוֹרָלוֹת. Dir obj of נָפַל.

וַיִּפֹּל הַגּוֹרָל עַל־יוֹנָה. Narrative discourse—mainline.

וַיִּפֹּל. Qal *wayyiqtol* 3 m s from נָפַל. On the use of the verb in the Qal, see above. Most translations fail to acknowledge the three-fold repetition of the root נָפַל and its association with גּוֹרָל. Rightly so, the RSV, NRSV, NEB, JPS, and NAB all translate the final occurrence of נָפַל as "fell" or "singled out," yet in so doing, the rhetorical unity of the verse is disrupted. Three clauses are typical of folk narrative and appear frequently throughout Jonah (see 1:5). On the rhetorical significance of three clauses in folk narrative, see Trible, 1994, 137–38.

הַגּוֹרָל. Subject of נָפַל.

עַל־יוֹנָה. Locative sense of the preposition, but understood metaphorically.

1:8 וַיֹּאמְרוּ אֵלָיו הַגִּידָה־נָּא לָנוּ בַּאֲשֶׁר לְמִי־הָרָעָה הַזֹּאת לָנוּ מַה־מְּלַאכְתְּךָ וּמֵאַיִן תָּבוֹא מָה אַרְצֶךָ וְאֵי־מִזֶּה עַם אָתָּה:

וַיֹּאמְרוּ אֵלָיו. Narrative discourse—mainline. The verb אָמַר serves as a discourse switch cue.

וַיֹּאמְרוּ. Qal *wayyiqtol* 3 m p.

אֵלָיו. The prepositional phrase functions as a complement to the verb, marking out the goal of the saying process. Objective pronoun.

הַגִּידָה־נָּא לָנוּ. Embedded hortatory discourse—mainline. On the use of the imperative as a mainline verb in hortatory discourse, see 1:2.

הַגִּידָה־נָּא. Hiph impv 2 m s + vol *he* from נָגַד- particle of entreaty. The voluntative *he* frequently augments the singular masculine imperative form. Since the emphatic nature of the voluntative *he* appears non-discernible in the imperative, Joüon and Muraoka suggests that the emotive particle נָּא is coupled to the imperative in an effort to generate greater emphasis (143). (On the daghesh in נָּא, see GKC, 71–72 [*daghesh forte conjunctivum*]).

לָנוּ. The prepositional phrase functions as complement to the verb, with the preposition marking out the indirect object. Objective pronoun.

בַּאֲשֶׁר לְמִי־הָרָעָה הַזֹּאת לָנוּ. Embedded hortatory discourse—off-the-line. On the role of the verbless clause in hortatory discourse, see 1:7.

בַּאֲשֶׁר לְמִי־. This phrase is the expanded form of בְּשֶׁלְמִי; which appeared in 1:7. Because this same clause appeared earlier in verse 7, selected LXX texts (Sinaiticus and Vaticanus) have omitted the second occurrence of this phrase, perhaps assuming an unnecessary repetition of the question. Even though the two phrases are nearly identical, their location in the text suggests a subtle distinction. In verse 7, the sailors are speaking to each other (אִישׁ אֶל־רֵעֵהוּ), but in verse 8, the question is asked again, with the focus narrowed as a result of lots being cast. As Trible concludes, "Rather than being a gloss, the repeated words in 1:8 link incidents as they advance the plot" (Trible, 1994, 139).

הָרָעָה הַזֹּאת. See 1:7.

לָנוּ. See 1:7.

מַה־מְּלַאכְתְּךָ. Embedded hortatory discourse—off-the-line. On the role of the verbless clause in hortatory discourse, see 1:7.

מַה. Interrogative. Subject of unmarked verbal clause. Three additional short interrogative clauses follow in staccato fashion, with both the first and second as well as the third and fourth clauses being conjoined by a simple *waw*. The construction of the two sections mirrors one another, each beginning with מַה in a verbless clause, followed by a *waw* + adverbial interrogative. The absence of any linkage between the second and third clauses may serve to highlight the nature of the questions expressed in each. On the interrogative sentence, see AC, 187–88.

מְלַאכְתְּךָ. Predicate of unmarked verbless clause. Wolff suggests that semantically מְלַאכְתְּךָ may be not be referring to Jonah's occupation, but more significantly, to his particular task (114). Such a rendering appears to relate better to the nature of the second question ("from where do you come?").

וּמֵאַיִן תָּבוֹא. Embedded hortatory discourse—off-the-line. Although not verbless, this clause continues the scene setting function of the previous clause, as suggested by the *waw*.

תָּבוֹא. Qal *yiqtol* 2 m s. The construction מֵאַיִן תָּבוֹא is used elsewhere to determine the purpose or reason for one's travel (cf. Judg 17:9; 19:17; Sasson, 114).

מָה אַרְצֶךָ. Embedded hortatory discourse—off-the-line. On the role of the verbless clause in hortatory discourse, see 1:7.

מָה. Interrogative. Subject of unmarked verbless clause.

אַרְצֶךְ. Predicate of unmarked verbless clause. Possessive pronoun.

וְאֵי־מִזֶּה עַם אָתָּה. Embedded hortatory discourse—off-the-line. On the role of the verbless clause in hortatory discourse, see 1:7.

וְאֵי־מִזֶּה. The entire construction has the sense of a "directional locative." Frequently such constructions are translated "from where" or "from which" (WO, 328). See also BDB, 262.

עַם. The word order in the final verbless clause is marked, with the predicate fronted. The emphasis then focuses on Jonah's "people."

אָתָּה. Subject of marked verbless clause.

1:9 וַיֹּאמֶר אֲלֵהֶם עִבְרִי אָנֹכִי וְאֶת־יְהוָֹה אֱלֹהֵי
הַשָּׁמַיִם אֲנִי יָרֵא אֲשֶׁר־עָשָׂה אֶת־הַיָּם וְאֶת־הַיַּבָּשָׁה:

וַיֹּאמֶר אֲלֵהֶם. Narrative discourse—mainline. The verb אָמַר serves as a discourse switch cue.

וַיֹּאמֶר. Qal wayyiqtol 3 m s.

אֲלֵהֶם. The prepositional phrase functions as a complement to the verb, marking out the goal of the saying process. Objective pronoun.

עִבְרִי אָנֹכִי. Embedded expository discourse—mainline. The response of Jonah comes in the form of an embedded expository discourse. This form of discourse seeks to explain or argue a thesis, and it is carried out primarily through verbless clauses.

עִבְרִי. Predicate of the verbless clause. Waltke and O'Connor note that when the predicate of a verbless clause is definite, the clause may be understood as a clause of identification (130–31). More recently, however, Buth has suggested, based on a generative-functional approach, that the underlying order in verbless clauses is Subject-Predicate, with the subject being identified as the more definite constituent. Any deviation from this order moves something to the first position in the clause, creating a focus on the fronted element (79–108). Just as the sailors' final question appears in a marked verbless clause, so too does Jonah's opening statement.

Jonah's initial retort responds to the last question of the sailors—a rhetorical device known as *hysteron proteron* (lit., "the latter as the former"; Trible, 1994, 140).

אָנֹכִי. Subject of marked verbless clause.

וְאֶת־יְהוָה אֱלֹהֵי הַשָּׁמַיִם אֲנִי יָרֵא. Embedded expository discourse—mainline. A second verbless clause signals the continuation of expository discourse.

וְאֶת־יְהוָה. The verbless clause is marked, with the object being fronted. Jonah's ethnic identity was fronted in the first clause, and the identity of Jonah's deity is fronted in the second.

אֱלֹהֵי הַשָּׁמַיִם. The construct relationship may be understood as expressing an adverbial relationship, with the location or origin of the construct noun indicated by the absolute noun (MNK, 199). The phrase stands in apposition to יְהוָה.

אֲנִי. Subject of verbless clause.

יָרֵא. Qal act ptc. The participle may be used to establish a durative circumstance, exhibiting "its adjectival origin in its essential use to express circumstances, states of affairs, facts, etc., rather than events" (WO, 624).

אֲשֶׁר־עָשָׂה אֶת־הַיָּם וְאֶת־הַיַּבָּשָׁה. Embedded expository discourse—off-the-line. The clause is a relative clause, and as such, offers background information. *Qatal* verbs in dependent clauses provide background information in expository discourse. The entire relative clause has been separated from the noun it modifies, יְהוָה. The separating of the attributive clause from the term being modified is known as *hyperbaton* (Trible, 1994, 141).

אֲשֶׁר־עָשָׂה. Rel pronoun – Qal *qatal* 3 m s.

אֶת־הַיָּם. Direct object of עָשָׂה.

וְאֶת־הַיַּבָּשָׁה. Although separated by the Jonah's claim, אֲנִי יָרֵא, the three terms הַיָּם, הַשָּׁמַיִם, and הַיַּבָּשָׁה function together to constitute a merismus, announcing the cosmic rule of יְהוָה. Such a proclamation only heightens the absurdity of Jonah's own desire to "flee" (v 3) from the presence of God.

1:10 וַיִּירְאוּ הָאֲנָשִׁים יִרְאָה גְדוֹלָה וַיֹּאמְרוּ אֵלָיו מַה־זֹּאת עָשִׂיתָ כִּי־יָדְעוּ הָאֲנָשִׁים כִּי־מִלִּפְנֵי יְהוָה הוּא בֹרֵחַ כִּי הִגִּיד לָהֶם:

וַיִּירְאוּ הָאֲנָשִׁים יִרְאָה גְדוֹלָה. Narrative discourse—mainline.

וַיִּירְאוּ. Qal *wayyiqtol* 3 m p.

הָאֲנָשִׁים. Subject of וַיִּירְאוּ. Throughout the remainder of the chapter, the individuals on the sailing vessel are no longer called "sailors" (הַמַּלָּחִים), but "men." The shift in nomenclature may have been intended to "flatten" any sense of disparity between the sailors and Jonah.

יִרְאָה גְדוֹלָה. The noun is an internal adjunct (often referred to as a *schema etymologicum, figura etymologica*, internal object, or internal accusative). The function of such a construction is to describe the intensity of the verbal idea. Although the noun stands as an object of the verb, it should not be translated as a direct object, "the men feared a great fear." Instead, it should be understood adverbially, "the men feared greatly." An internal adjunct is frequently modified by an attributive adjective (AC, 15–16). The author makes extensive use of internal adjuncts throughout the book, heightening the intensity of the language.

וַיֹּאמְרוּ אֵלָיו. Narrative discourse—mainline.

וַיֹּאמְרוּ. Qal *wayyiqtol* 3 m p. The verb serves as a discourse switch cue. See 1:6.

אֵלָיו. The prepositional phrase functions as a complement to the verb, marking out the goal of the saying process. Objective pronoun.

מַה־זֹּאת עָשִׂיתָ. Embedded expository discourse—off-the-line. The X + *qatal* construction moves the clause off the mainline.

מַה־זֹּאת. The interrogative is often coupled with the demonstrative pronoun זֶה or זֹאת to introduce exclamatory statements (GKC, 471). The demonstrative pronoun is anaphoric, referring to the prior events. The explanatory nature of the subsequent clause reinforces the reference.

עָשִׂיתָ. Qal *qatal* 2 m s from עָשָׂה. The conjoining of מַה־זֹּאת with the *qatal* of עָשָׂה appears frequently in narrative texts with עָשָׂה appearing most frequently in the 2 m s form (Gen 3:13; 12:18; 26:10; 29:25; Exod 14:11; Judg 15:11). The exclamatory statement stands between two irreconcilable elements in the narrative. The sailors heard Jonah's confession in verse 9 (אֲנִי יָרֵא), but apparently prior to that (as indicated in the remainder of verse 10), they had been told of Jonah's fleeing from Yahweh. Hence, מַה־זֹּאת עָשִׂיתָ is not a question meant to result in information; it is a response reflecting the astonishment of the men (Wolff, 116; Sasson, 120).

כִּי־יָדְעוּ הָאֲנָשִׁים. Narrative discourse—off-the-line. Hebrew typically embeds one discourse type in another through the use of a subordinating particle (כִּי). In this case, the narrator has embedded narrative discourse within expository discourse, briefly interrupting the flow of direct speech. Within narrative discourse a *qatal* in a dependent clause provides background information, particularly backgrounded action. An embedded discourse has a significant function for the discourse in which it is embedded (Garrett, 321). Beyond simply supplying background information, the embedded narrative

provides the rationale for the exclamatory comment מַה־זֹּאת עָשִׂיתָ.
On the function of background clauses, see van Wolde, 39.

יָדְעוּ. Qal *qatal* 3 m p.

הָאֲנָשִׁים. Subj of יָדְעוּ.

כִּי־מִלִּפְנֵי יְהוָה הוּא בֹרֵחַ. Embedded narrative discourse—off-
the-line. When כִּי introduces a subordinate clause following the verb
יָדַע, then the entire clause functions as an object clause, resulting in
the particle being translated as the subordinating conjunction "that."

כִּי־מִלִּפְנֵי יְהוָה. See 1:2. The subordinate clause is marked, with
the prepositional phrase מִלִּפְנֵי יְהוָה fronted. The plight of the sailors
and Jonah was not because Jonah had fled, it was because Jonah had
fled from Yahweh.

הוּא בֹרֵחַ. Qal act ptc. On the durative function of the participle,
see 1:9.

כִּי הִגִּיד לָהֶם. Embedded narrative discourse—off-the-line. When
the main clause (יָדְעוּ הָאֲנָשִׁים) is followed by כִּי, the particle marks a
causal clause meant to provide a reason for the current state of affairs.

כִּי. In such a construction, כִּי is understood as a coordinating conjunction and should be translated "because."

הִגִּיד. Hiph *qatal* 3 m s from נָגַד. When a *qatal* appears in a causal
clause and the verb in the main clause pertains to a past event or circumstance, then the *qatal* in the causal clause should be rendered as a
past perfect (WO, 490).

לָהֶם. The prepositional phrase functions as a complement to the
verb, with the preposition marking the indirect object. Objective pronoun.

1:11 וַיֹּאמְרוּ אֵלָיו מַה־נַּעֲשֶׂה לָּךְ וְיִשְׁתֹּק הַיָּם מֵעָלֵינוּ כִּי
הַיָּם הוֹלֵךְ וְסֹעֵר׃

וַיֹּאמְרוּ אֵלָיו. Narrative discourse—mainline. The presence of a *wayyiqtol* shifts the discourse from off-the-line to mainline, thus moving the plotline forward, as opposed to the three previous clauses that were narrative discourse, but off-the-line, simply providing background information.

וַיֹּאמְרוּ. Qal *wayyiqtol* 3 m p. On the use of אָמַר as a discourse switch cue, see 1:6.

אֵלָיו. The prepositional phrase functions as a complement to the verb, marking out the goal of the saying process.

מַה־נַּעֲשֶׂה לָּךְ. Embedded hortatory discourse—off-the-line.

מַה־נַּעֲשֶׂה. Interr – Qal *yiqtol* 1c p. The X + *yiqtol* construction signals topicalization, hence producing a marked clause. מַה is cataphoric, pointing forward to its referent (the response of Jonah) in verse 12.

לָּךְ. *Lamed* of interest. Objective pronoun. Normally a preposition conjoined with 2 m s suffix would appear as לְךָ. In this verse, however, the construction appears as לָּךְ, a pausal form that is indicated by the presence of the *zaqeph qaton*. The unusual doubling of the *lamed* is the result of the close juncture of two words—in this case נַּעֲשֶׂה and לָּךְ. Such a phenomenon may be labeled a *daghesh euphonicum* (GKC, 71), or more generally, a conjunctive *daghesh* (JM, 79–80).

וְיִשְׁתֹּק הַיָּם מֵעָלֵינוּ. Embedded hortatory discourse—off-the-line. The *yiqtol* functions modally in hortatory discourse. When a *waw* copulative + *yiqtol* follows a question, the second clause expresses a sense of purpose, "in order that."

וְיִשְׁתֹּק. *Waw* cop + Qal *yiqtol* 3 m s. Since the verb is functioning modally, the translation should attempt to convey the sense of possibility ("might").

הַיָּם. Subject of וְיִשְׁתֹּק.

מֵעָלֵינוּ. The construction implies a comprehensive locative sense (i.e., "around"; WO, 216). Objective pronoun.

כִּי הַיָּם הוֹלֵךְ וְסֹעֵר. Embedded hortatory discourse—off-the-line.

כִּי. When the particle כִּי marks a clause that offers the actual reason for the state of affairs, then it is understood as a coordinating conjunction, introducing a causal clause.

הַיָּם. Subject of the clause.

הוֹלֵךְ וְסֹעֵר. Qal act ptc + *waw* cop + Qal act ptc. When functioning as a verb, participles can note action that is imminent. Although the storm itself is not new to the narrative (v 4), the impending intensity of the storm appears to be the rationale for the question asked by the sailors. Thus the verb should be translated with an ingressive sense. The verb הָלַךְ is often employed in an auxiliary capacity to convey a sense of continuance (GKC, 344). Coupled with סָעַר the two verbs form a hendiadys meant to suggest the growing strength and intensity of the storm (Sasson, 123).

1:12 וַיֹּאמֶר אֲלֵיהֶם שָׂאוּנִי וַהֲטִילֻנִי אֶל־הַיָּם וְיִשְׁתֹּק הַיָּם
מֵעֲלֵיכֶם כִּי יוֹדֵעַ אָנִי כִּי בְשֶׁלִּי הַסַּעַר הַגָּדוֹל הַזֶּה
עֲלֵיכֶם:

וַיֹּאמֶר אֲלֵיהֶם. Narrative discourse—mainline.

וַיֹּאמֶר. Qal *wayyiqtol* 3 m p. On אָמַר as a discourse switch cue, see 1:6.

אֲלֵיהֶם. The prepositional phrase functions as a complement to the verb, marking out the goal of the saying process. Objective pronoun.

שָׂאוּנִי. Embedded hortatory discourse—mainline. The return to imperative verb forms signals the return to hortatory discourse. Although one might be tempted to consider the discourse as instructional (Jonah instructing the sailors to throw him overboard), the language is hortatory. Jonah attempts to persuade the sailors to throw him overboard—their initial reluctance further confirms the nature of the discourse. Qal impv 2 m p from נָשָׂא + 1 c s suf. The pronominal suffix stands as a complement to the verb, indicating the direct object.

וַהֲטִילֻנִי אֶל־הַיָּם. Embedded hortatory discourse—mainline.

וַהֲטִילֻנִי. Waw cop + Hiph impv 2 m p from טוּל + 1 c s suf. The waw copulative is used when two imperatives imply the same addressee. The pronominal suffix stands as a complement to the verb, indicating the direct object.

אֶל־הַיָּם. The preposition carries a terminative sense, marking movement "into" something.

וְיִשְׁתֹּק הַיָּם מֵעֲלֵיכֶם. Embedded hortatory discourse—off-the-line. See 1:11.

וְיִשְׁתֹּק. Waw cop + Qal yiqtol 3 m s. As in verse 11, the construction creates a consecutive clause, except that in this verse the construction is preceded by an imperative.

הַיָּם. Subject of וְיִשְׁתֹּק.

מֵעֲלֵיכֶם. See 1:11.

כִּי יוֹדֵעַ אָנִי. Embedded hortatory discourse—off-the-line. The particle כִּי functions as a coordinating conjunction, introducing a causal clause.

כִּי. Coordinating conjunction.

יוֹדֵעַ אָנִי. Qal act ptc – 1 c s pronoun. The unmarked word order, noun + participle, has been reversed in this clause, suggesting the narrator's emphasis on Jonah's awareness. The Masoretes observed the emphasis and placed a pausal accent (zaqeph qaton) over אָנִי, drawing additional attention to the construction. Sasson suggests that יָדַע can "carry a legal sense, 'to recognize,' 'to know,' 'to admit,' when accepting or entertaining a legal decision" (125). The emphatic construction proves to be an acknowledgment of responsibility, thus absolving the sailors of guilt for following the directives in the previous clause.

כִּי בְשֶׁלִּי הַסַּעַר הַגָּדוֹל הַזֶּה עֲלֵיכֶם. Embedded hortatory discourse—off-the-line. The discourse remains off-the-line as the clause provides additional explanatory information.

כִּי. Subordinate conj. On the use of כִּי in introducing an object clause with the verb יָדַע, see 1:10.

בְשֶׁלִּי. Prep + rel pronoun + prep + 1 c s suf. See 1:7 for a similar construction (there an interrogative pronoun appears in place of the 1 c s suffix). Just as the narrator inverted the previous clause for emphasis, so too does the narrator invert the final clause in the verse. By fronting the prepositional phrase, the narrator retains the focus on Jonah and his admission of culpability.

הַסַּעַר הַגָּדוֹל הַזֶּה. The same phrase for the tempest (הַגָּדוֹל הַסַּעַר) appears in 1:4, connecting the beginning of the narrative with the culminating events. Attributive use of demonstrative pronoun.

עֲלֵיכֶם. Locative sense of the preposition. Objective pronoun.

Jonah 1:13-16

[13]And the men desperately rowed in order to return to dry land, but they were not able because the sea was growing stormier around them. [14]And then they cried out to the LORD, "Please O LORD, do not let us perish because of the life of this man, and do not put innocent blood on us. You are the LORD; you have acted as you have desired." [15]Then they lifted up Jonah and they hurled him into the sea, and the sea ceased from its raging. [16]Then the men feared the LORD even more and they offered a sacrifice to the LORD and they made vows.

וַיַּחְתְּרוּ הָאֲנָשִׁים לְהָשִׁיב אֶל־הַיַּבָּשָׁה וְלֹא יָכֹלוּ כִּי 1:13
הַיָּם הוֹלֵךְ וְסֹעֵר עֲלֵיהֶם:

וַיַּחְתְּרוּ הָאֲנָשִׁים. Narrative discourse—mainline. The *wayyiqtol* serves as a discourse switch cue, moving the text from hortatory to narrative discourse.

וַיַּחְתְּרוּ. Qal *wayyiqtol* 3 m p. In other contexts, the verb suggests digging (Am 9:2) or illicit entry into a house (Job 24:16; Jer 2:24). Often such action is considered futile (Ps 139:6), perhaps contributing additionally to the meaning of the word in Jonah. The translation above attempts to capture both notions.

הָאֲנָשִׁים. Subject of וַיַּחְתְּרוּ.

לְהָשִׁיב אֶל־הַיַּבָּשָׁה. Narrative discourse—mainline. The infinitive construct with a לְ indicates a subordinate purpose clause meant to explain the statements in the mainline clause.

לְהָשִׁיב. Prep + Hiph inf constr from שׁוּב. The לְ (*lamed* of purpose) + infinitive introduces a purpose clause. The subject of the main clause (הָאֲנָשִׁים) serves as the subject of the purpose clause as well.

אֶל־הַיַּבָּשָׁה. The preposition carries a locational sense, but takes on directional connotations (AC, 98). Thus, the preposition is understood as marking movement towards an object. The phrase אֶל־הַיַּבָּשָׁה is found only here and in Jonah 2:11 (also with a terminative sense), where the fish vomits Jonah אֶל־הַיַּבָּשָׁה.

וְלֹא יָכֹלוּ. Narrative discourse—off-the-line. Although the negative particle creates a low-ranking clause in the narrative profile scheme (stating what does *not* occur versus what does), the clause is no less important. The negated verb actually begins to move the narrative to the culminating scene in verse 15. Waw cop + neg part – Qal *qatal* 3 c p. Note the disjunctive use of the *waw*.

כִּי הַיָּם הוֹלֵךְ וְסֹעֵר עֲלֵיהֶם. Narrative—off-the-line. The particle כִּי functions as a coordinating conjunction, introducing a causal clause. The clause is off-the-line because it provides background information related to the previous clause.

כִּי. See 1:11.

הַיָּם. See 1:11

הוֹלֵךְ וְסֹעֵר. See 1:11.

עֲלֵיהֶם. Locative sense of the preposition. Objective pronoun.

1:14 וַיִּקְרְאוּ אֶל־יְהוָה וַיֹּאמְרוּ אָנָּה יְהוָה אַל־נָא נֹאבְדָה
בְּנֶפֶשׁ הָאִישׁ הַזֶּה וְאַל־תִּתֵּן עָלֵינוּ דָּם נָקִיא כִּי־אַתָּה
יְהוָה כַּאֲשֶׁר חָפַצְתָּ עָשִׂיתָ׃

וַיִּקְרְאוּ אֶל־יְהוָה. Narrative discourse—mainline.

וַיִּקְרְאוּ. Qal *wayyiqtol* 3 m p. The verb קָרָא is frequently employed in a quotative frame (73 times). Although it may stand alone (9 times) or with the infinitive form of אָמַר (7), קָרָא more often appears as part of a multiple-verb frame (57 times). In such cases, the second verb appears in a finite form, matching the first with respect to gender and number. Miller suggests that "the central configuration for קָרָא is in multiple-verb frames, where it is used most often in prototypically dialogic contexts" (Miller, 2003, 336). Further, Miller suggests that the final verb carries the least metapragmatic information, with the first verb presenting the significant features of the speech event (331–40). The multiple-verb frame אָמַר . . . קָרָא is frequently the quotative frame that introduces the cry of humans to God (Miller, 334 n. 42).

אֶל־יְהוָה. The prepositional phrase functions as a complement to the verb, marking out the goal of the saying process.

וַיֹּאמְרוּ. Narrative discourse—mainline. On אָמַר as a discourse switch cue, see 1:6.

אָנָּה יְהוָה אַל־נָא נֹאבְדָה בְּנֶפֶשׁ הָאִישׁ הַזֶּה. Embedded hortatory discourse—off-the-line.

אָנָּה יְהוָה. Particle of entreaty—proper noun. אָנָּה frequently appears at the opening of laments, suggesting the tenor of the prayer. As Sasson has observed, this particle (אָנָּה) uses a volitive when "it aims to withhold or to cancel a threatened action" (132). The particle itself appears eleven times in the Hebrew Bible, seven times with a א as the final letter and 4 times with a ה in the final position.

The proper name, יְהוָה, is a vocative, following the particle of entreaty. Such a construction is frequent in addresses or petitions. Although vocatives most often appear in direct speech discourse and stand in apposition to either a second person pronoun or the "built-in" subject of an imperative, they may also stand as syntactically separate from the clause, and hence regarded as an adjunct (MNK, 249). The vocative appears as an adjunct in the present circumstance.

אַל־נָא. Neg – particle of entreaty. The particle of entreaty is frequently associated with volitional forms, often appearing after the verb. When אַל is used for negation, however, the particle will appear between the term of negation and the verb itself.

נֹאבְדָה. Qal yiqtol 1 c p + coh he.

בְּנֶפֶשׁ הָאִישׁ הַזֶּה. The preposition indicates cause—the so-called beth causa. The phrase נֶפֶשׁ הָאִישׁ occurs only one other place in the Hebrew Bible (Prov 13:8). The more preferred construction is with הָאָדָם in the absolute position of the construct phrase. The unusual construction may once again demonstrate the author's penchant to deviate from expected Hebrew norms. Attributive use of the demonstrative pronoun.

וְאַל־תִּתֵּן עָלֵינוּ דָּם נָקִיא. Embedded hortatory discourse—off-the-line. Although not an imperative (the mainline of hortatory discourse), the אַל + *yiqtol* construction signals a prohibitive command that nearly carries the same force as that of the mainline verb forms (on the use of mitigation in hortatory discourse, see Rocine, 110–11).

וְאַל־תִּתֵּן. *Waw* cop + neg – Qal *yiqtol* 2 m s from נָתַן.

עָלֵינוּ. The prepositional phrase functions as a complement to the verb, with the preposition marking the indirect object. The preposition עַל is understood metaphorically when speaking of a burden or a duty placed upon an individual (WO, 217).

דָּם נָקִיא. In the present construction, the adjective serves to modify the noun, and hence is translated as "innocent blood." But as Sasson has noted, there are cases elsewhere in the Hebrew Bible where דָּם loses its accent and enters into a construct relationship with the nominalized adjective (דַּם נָקִיא). In such constructions, the translation is better rendered "blood of the innocent person," with the emphasis on the blamelessness of the victim. But in Jonah, such a construction does not appear, thus rendering the phrase "innocent blood" with the emphasis on the (innocent) act of shedding blood (Sasson, 134).

כִּי־אַתָּה יְהוָה. Embedded expository discourse—mainline. The particle כִּי can signal that one discourse type has been embedded within another. The presence of a verbless clause following the particle serves as a discourse switch cue, moving the narrative from hortatory to expository discourse. The translation actually has divided the two forms of discourse creating a second sentence out of the verbless clause in an effort to signal a shift. Although the embedded discourse is subordinate to the larger discourse in which it is found, the embedded discourse can, and often does, figure prominently in the overall text. In the verbless clause, the sailors issue an unsolicited confession, absolving them of any guilt for the events in verse 15.

כַּאֲשֶׁר חָפַצְתָּ עָשִׂיתָ. Embedded expository discourse—off-the-line. A *qatal* in a dependent clause is meant to offer background information to verbless clauses.

כַּאֲשֶׁר. כַּאֲשֶׁר may be used to introduce a comparative clause. In such clauses the most common construction is כַּאֲשֶׁר + protasis— כֵּן + apodosis (WO, 641). The absence of כֵּן in the apodosis is the result of ellipsis.

חָפַצְתָּ. Qal *qatal* 2 m s.

עָשִׂיתָ. Qal *qatal* 2 m s. The statement is not an affirmation of Yahweh's sovereignty (contra Sasson, 135–36). If the clause is understood as an off-the-line construction, then its purpose is to provide background information. Thus the referent to the clause must be in the relative past (relative to the mainline). The verse opens with the men pleading that they not perish בְּנֶפֶשׁ הָאִישׁ הַזֶּה, followed by the request that they not be held accountable for דָּם נָקִיא. The basis of both requests is the casting of the lots (v 7), in which Yahweh "has acted as he has desired." The apparent question is not whether Yahweh has the power to act as he wishes, but whether the sailors will be held responsible for what they perceive as Yahweh's choice via the lots. The appeal to casting of the lots is meant to secure the answer for the sailors. The JPS translation comes close to capturing such a nuance by rendering the final two clauses as "For You, O LORD, by your will, have brought this about."

1:15   וַיִּשְׂאוּ אֶת־יוֹנָה וַיְטִלֻהוּ אֶל־הַיָּם וַיַּעֲמֹד הַיָּם מִזַּעְפּוֹ:

וַיִּשְׂאוּ אֶת־יוֹנָה. Narrative discourse—mainline. The *wayyiqtol* verb serves as a discourse switch cue, moving the text from expository discourse to narrative discourse.

וַיִּשְׂאוּ. Qal *wayyiqtol* 3 m p from נָשָׂא.

אֶת־יוֹנָה. Direct object.

וַיְטִלֻהוּ אֶל־הַיָּם. Narrative discourse—mainline.

וַיְטִלֻהוּ. Hiph *wayyiqtol* 3 m p from טוּל + 3 m s suf. The pronominal suffix stands as a complement to the verb, indicating the direct object. The language in 1:4 and the language in 1:15 operate as an *inclusio* for the entire "sea" pericope. What begin when Yahweh הֵטִיל רוּחַ־גְּדוֹלָה אֶל־הַיָּם is resolved when וַיְטִלֻהוּ אֶל־הַיָּם.

אֶל־הַיָּם. See 1:5.

וַיַּעֲמֹד הַיָּם מִזַּעְפּוֹ. Narrative discourse—mainline.

וַיַּעֲמֹד. Qal *wayyiqtol* 3 m s.

הַיָּם. Subject of וַיַּעֲמֹד. The attribution of human activity to an inanimate object appears again in verse 15. Just as the narrative begins with the use of prosopopoeia in 1:5 to highlight the activity of the ship, the narrative concludes with another example of prosopopoeia, but with יָם as the inanimate subject.

מִזַּעְפּוֹ. The noun זַעַף occurs only six times, three referring to human anger (Prov 19:12; 2 Chron 16:10; 28:9) and two referring to divine rage (Is 30:30; Mi 7:9). Jonah 1:15 is the only example of the term being applied to an inanimate object, furthering the propospoetic nature of the text. Possessive pronoun.

1:16 וַיִּירְאוּ הָאֲנָשִׁים יִרְאָה גְדוֹלָה אֶת־יְהוָה וַיִּזְבְּחוּ־זֶבַח
לַיהוָה וַיִּדְּרוּ נְדָרִים:

וַיִּירְאוּ הָאֲנָשִׁים יִרְאָה גְדוֹלָה אֶת־יְהוָה. Narrative discourse—mainline. Sequential sense of *wayyiqtol*.

וַיִּירְאוּ. Qal *wayyiqtol* 3 m p.

הָאֲנָשִׁים. Subject of וַיִּירְאוּ.

יִרְאָה גְדוֹלָה. The noun is an internal adjunct. See 1:10.

אֶת־יְהוָה. Direct object of וַיִּירְאוּ.

וַיִּזְבְּחוּ־זֶבַח לַיהוָה‎. Narrative discourse—mainline.

וַיִּזְבְּחוּ־זֶבַח‎. Qal *wayyiqtol* 3 m p – m p noun. The noun functions as an internal adjunct. In the previous clause, the internal adjunct intensified the meaning of the verbal idea. In this instance, however, the internal adjunct appears to have no semantic meaning (MNK, 245).

לַיהוָה‎. The prepositional phrase is a complement to the verb, with the preposition marking the indirect object. See 1:6.

וַיִּדְּרוּ נְדָרִים‎. Narrative discourse—mainline. A *wayyiqtol* may be used, albeit rarely, to indicate simultaneous events (cf. Gen 45:2). The context does not suggest sequential acts, but more likely simultaneous acts, predicated upon the first clause וַיִּירְאוּ הָאֲנָשִׁים יִרְאָה גְדוֹלָה אֶת־יְהוָה‎.

וַיִּדְּרוּ‎. Qal *wayyiqtol* 3 m p from נָדַר‎.

נְדָרִים‎. The noun functions as an internal adjunct, with no apparent semantic meaning. In noting the structure of verse 16, Trible observes the length of each clause from five words, to three words, and finally to two words. Rhetorically, such a structure moves the sailors from the scene.

Jonah 2:1-10

¹And then the LORD appointed a great fish to swallow Jonah and Jonah was in the belly of the fish three days and three nights. ²Then Jonah prayed to the LORD his God from the belly of the fish. ³And then he said,

> "I cried out to the LORD from my distress,
>> And he answered me.
>> From the belly of Sheol, I cried,
>> You heard my voice.
> ⁴You cast me into the deep,
>> into the heart of the seas,
>> so that deep currents began surrounding me.

All your waves and billows passed over me.
⁵But then I said, "I am banished
   From before your eyes.
Nevertheless I will continue to look
   To your holy temple."
⁶The waters enclosed over me up to the neck,
   The deeps began surrounding me,
Seaweed was bound to my head.
⁷To the bottom of the mountains, I went down.
   The underworld, its bars, closed behind me forever.
You brought up my life from the Pit,
   O LORD, my God.
⁸When my life was fainting within me,
   I remembered the LORD
And my prayer came to you in your holy temple.
⁹Those who worship completely worthless objects
   disregard their covenant loyalty.
¹⁰But I, with a thankful voice,
   will sacrifice to you.
That which I have vowed, I will pay.
   Salvation belongs to the LORD.

וַיְמַ֤ן יְהוָה֙ דָּ֣ג גָּד֔וֹל לִבְלֹ֖עַ אֶת־יוֹנָ֑ה וַיְהִ֤י יוֹנָה֙ בִּמְעֵ֣י   2:1
הַדָּ֔ג שְׁלֹשָׁ֥ה יָמִ֖ים וּשְׁלֹשָׁ֥ה לֵילֽוֹת

וַיְמַ֤ן יְהוָה֙ דָּ֣ג גָּד֔וֹל. Narrative discourse—mainline.

וַיְמַ֤ן. Qal *wayyiqtol* 3 m s מָנָה.

יְהוָה. Subject of וַיְמַ֤ן.

דָּ֣ג גָּד֔וֹל. Direct object of וַיְמַ֤ן. The use of the adjective גָּדוֹל
creates a word play with the noun דָּג; the consonants are reversed,
דָּג and גָּד(וֹל).

לִבְלֹעַ אֶת־יוֹנָה. Narrative discourse—mainline. The infinitive + לְ introduces an subordinate purpose clause (WO, 606–7; JM, 633–34).

לִבְלֹעַ. Prep + Qal inf constr.

אֶת־יוֹנָה. Direct object of inf constr.

וַיְהִי יוֹנָה בִּמְעֵי הַדָּג שְׁלֹשָׁה יָמִים וּשְׁלֹשָׁה לֵילוֹת. Narrative discourse—mainline. When וַיְהִי appears in the course of a scene, it "signals that a state of affairs needs to be treated on par with the mainstream of the narration" (MNK, 333). Thus the verb should not be understood as a type of discourse marker (cf. 1:1; 3:1).

וַיְהִי. Qal *wayyiqtol* 3 m s from הָיָה.

יוֹנָה. Subject of וַיְהִי.

בִּמְעֵי הַדָּג. The preposition בְּ indicates spatial localization—the so-called *beth locale*.

שְׁלֹשָׁה יָמִים וּשְׁלֹשָׁה לֵילוֹת. The nouns serve as adjuncts, indicating time. When the cardinal numbers three through ten modify an indefinite noun, they will differ in gender, remain in the absolute state, and precede the noun it modifies. Although לֵילוֹת possesses a feminine plural ending, the noun לַיְלָה is masculine, hence וּשְׁלֹשָׁה לֵילוֹת is grammatically consistent.

2:2   וַיִּתְפַּלֵּל יוֹנָה אֶל־יְהוָה אֱלֹהָיו מִמְּעֵי הַדָּגָה:

Narrative discourse—mainline.

וַיִּתְפַּלֵּל. Hithpael *wayyiqtol* 3 m s.

יוֹנָה. Subject of וַיִּתְפַּלֵּל.

אֶל־יְהוָה אֱלֹהָיו. The prepositional phrase functions as a complement to the verb, with the preposition marking the indirect object. אֱלֹהָיו stands in apposition to יְהוָה, serving to identify the leadword.

The use of the 3 m s suffix in אֱלֹהָיו, while unusual, is "frequent in Hebrew especially when major personalities are brought into intimate colloquy with God" (Sasson, 155). See, for example, Exodus 32:11 (Moses); 1 Samuel 30:6 (David); 1 Kings 11:4 (Solomon); 2 Kings 5:11 (Elisha). A similar construction (יְהוָה אֱלֹהָי) appears later in the psalm itself, thus connecting, in part, the frame of the psalm with what some consider to be the central or core affirmation of the psalm itself (Christensen, 226–28).

מִמְּעֵי הַדָּגָה. The feminine form of fish, הַדָּגָה, has elicited considerable discussion, particularly given that the masculine form appears in 2:1 and 2:11. Although there are several Hebrew words that may be either masculine or feminine, דָּג is not one of them. Gesenius suggests that Jonah 2:2 is example of a *nomen unitatis*, or a singulative, in which one gender expresses the collective unit, while the other appears to indicate a single component within that unit (GKC, 394; see also WO, 105). Although such a phenomenon appears in 1:3 with the use of אֲנִיָּה (the masculine form אֳנִי is the collective noun), it does not seem to explain the irregularity in 2:2. Sasson suggests an alternative explanation. Sasson notes that in the Hebrew the singular form of a word can be used instead of its plural form, providing that the number (singular vs. plural) is not the main point of the text (156; see GKC 395 for examples). A similar phenomenon occurs with masculine words supplanting feminine words (GKC 390). Thus Sasson concludes, "I do not think that such blurring of gender is really a grammatical issue; more likely it is a vernacular or narratological one. A storyteller could simply use either gender for the animal—or both at once—when the sex of the animal was of no importance to the tale" (156). One may be better served by Trible's conclusion that the shift in gender is "inexplicable" (158).

2:3   וַיֹּאמֶר

קָרָאתִי מִצָּרָה לִי   אֶל־יְהוָה וַיַּעֲנֵנִי
מִבֶּטֶן שְׁאוֹל שִׁוַּעְתִּי   שָׁמַעְתָּ קוֹלִי׃

וַיֹּאמֶר. Narrative discourse—mainline. On the use of אָמַר as a discourse switch cue, see 1:6. Qal *wayyiqtol* 3 m s.

קָרָאתִי מִצָּרָה לִי אֶל־יְהוָה. Expository discourse—off-the-line. With the appearance of אָמַר, the discourse switches from narrative discourse to a form of direct speech, namely, expository speech. The expository discourse, however, begins with an embedded oral narrative, hence, moving the discourse off-the-line. The narrative provides a rationale for the primary theme or thesis of the expository discourse (v 10). Typically the *wayyiqtol* serves as the main verb form in narrative discourse, but in oral narrative discourse, the *qatal* is clause initial (Rocine, 149–50; Niccacci, 41–43).

קָרָאתִי. Qal *qatal* 1 c s. Much of the language of Jonah's psalm echoes the language of the Psalter (Magonet, 44–49), and Line A of verse 3 is no doubt from Psalm 120:1. In that psalm, however, the verb קָרָאתִי appears later in the verse, just before וַיַּעֲנֵנִי. Wolff explains that it may have been moved to the front of the verse in Jonah 2:3 for emphasis (134). The shift in position appears better explained given the observations of discourse analysis (see above). The idiom קָרָא אֶל is frequently employed in Jonah when one invokes the Deity.

מִצָּרָה. The preposition functions spatially, indicating the place from where an action is undertaken.

לִי. The prepositional phrase functions adjectively, indicating possession. Objective pronoun.

אֶל־יְהוָה. The prepositional phrase functions as a complement to the verb, with the preposition marking the indirect object.

וַיַּעֲנֵנִי. Expository discourse—off-the-line. The presence of a *wayyiqtol* signals the continuation of the embedded narrative discourse. Although the discourse began with a clause initial *qatal*, it proceeds using the expected patterns of narrative discourse. Qal *wayyiqtol* 3 m s + 1 c s suffix. Objective pronoun.

מִבֶּטֶן שְׁאוֹל שִׁוַּעְתִּי. Expository discourse—off-the-line. מִבֶּטֶן שְׁאוֹל is fronted, producing an X + *qatal* construction. Line A usually follows the norms of Hebrew syntax, but Line B may be altered by the poet for stylistic reasons. As Garr has suggested, "having composed a complete sentence in the first half of the poetic line, the poet then proceeds to manipulate both its content and grammar in the second" (69). In this case, in addition to fronting "from the belly of Sheol," the sequence change produces a partial chiasmus; Line A can be expressed as A B C, with Line B being expressed as B' A' C'. In addition, the fronting of מִבֶּטֶן שְׁאוֹל produces alliteration in Line B, with a three-fold repetition of the שׁ.

מִבֶּטֶן שְׁאוֹל. The preposition functions spatially, indicating the place from where an action is undertaken. The noun stands in a construct relationship with שְׁאוֹל. The entire construct phrase indicates a relationship of possession, metaphorically expressing the relationship between a possession (body part) and the possessor (MNK, 198). The metaphor "belly of Sheol" is unique to Jonah, and as Sasson suggests, "the poet probably found it particularly appropriate to the context" given the mention of the fish's "belly" in 2:1 (172).

שִׁוַּעְתִּי. Piel *qatal* 1 c s.

שָׁמַעְתָּ קוֹלִי. Expository discourse—off-the-line. Continuation of embedded oral narrative discourse.

שָׁמַעְתָּ. Qal *qatal* 2 m s. Although the verb shifts to second person, semantically, it still remains parallel to וַיַּעֲנֵנִי.

קוֹלִי. Direct object of שָׁמַעְתָּ. Possessive pronoun.

2:4   וַתַּשְׁלִיכֵנִי מְצוּלָה בִּלְבַב יַמִּים   וְנָהָר יְסֹבְבֵנִי
        כָּל־מִשְׁבָּרֶיךָ וְגַלֶּיךָ   עָלַי עָבָרוּ:

וָאַתַּשְׁלִיכֵנִי מְצוּלָה בִּלְבַב יַמִּים. Expository discourse—off-the-line. Embedded oral narrative discourse continues with the *wayyiqtol*.

וָאַתַּשְׁלִיכֵנִי. Hiphil *wayyiqtol* 2 m s + 1 c s suffix. Objective pronoun. Although the verb form could be parsed as a 3 f s with מְצוּלָה as the subject (cf. Ps 69:16), the shift to second person in Line B of verse 3 as well as the second person possessive pronouns in Line B of verse 4 warrant against such a reading.

מְצוּלָה. The verb שָׁלַךְ is frequently followed by a preposition such as עַל, אֶל, or בְּ. Wolff suggests that the prepositional phrase בִּלְבַב יַמִּים fits the typical construction with the verb, thus leading him to conclude that מְצוּלָה is a "subsequent and additional interpretation" of "heart of the seas" (126). The syntactic function of מְצוּלָה indicates that the noun is probably not a secondary interpretation to the clause. With verbs of movement, nouns that are non-objects (not direct objects) may act as a complement to the verb (WO term this construction an accusative of place [169–70]). In such constructions, the verb is followed by another noun (absent a preposition) indicating place or location (cf. Gen 18:1; Gen 45:25; Isa 44:13).

בִּלְבַב יַמִּים. As an adjunct to the verb (וָאַתַּשְׁלִיכֵנִי), the prepositional phrase stands as an adverbial modifier.

וְנָהָר יְסֹבְבֵנִי. Expository discourse—off-the-line. The *waw* is understood as a subordinating conjunction, indicating that וְנָהָר יְסֹבְבֵנִי is the result of the action in the previous clause ("clause of result," Wolff, 127).

וְנָהָר. The noun frequently refers to a literal "river" or a "canal," but it may refer to underground streams (Job 28:11). Given the prepositional phrase בִּלְבַב יַמִּים earlier in the line, the notion of deep water currents seems most plausible (Simon, 20; Sasson, 175–76; Trible 164). Its fronted position may be meant to highlight the depths to which Jonah has sunk.

יְסֹבְבֵנִי. Polel *yiqtol* 3 m s + 1 c s suffix. The *yiqtol* form may be understood as having an "incipient past non-perfective" aspect.

Waltke and O'Connor explain that in this form "the speaker has in
view the initial and continuing phases within the internal temporal
structure of a past situation." Or put more succinctly, this use of the
yiqtol "combines the notions of commencement and continuation"
(203–4). The verb סָבַב can mean to enclose or envelop something,
but the more frequent meaning in the Polel is to encompass, in the
sense of protection (BDB, 686).

כָּל־מִשְׁבָּרֶיךָ וְגַלֶּיךָ עָלַי עָבָרוּ. Expository discourse—off-the-
line. Embedded oral narrative discourse continues. Within narrative
discourse X + *qatal* is a form of topicalization. Further, the present
clause is actually an example of double fronting: S + PP + V.

כָּל־מִשְׁבָּרֶיךָ וְגַלֶּיךָ. Subject of עָבָרוּ. The construct noun כָּל
governs a coordinate noun phrase. Possessive pronouns.

עָלַי. As an adjunct to the verb (עָבָרוּ), the prepositional phrase
stands as an adverbial modifier. Objective pronoun.

עָבָרוּ. Qal *qatal* 3 c p. Garr has noted that frequently in Hebrew
poetry, the verb in Line B appears in the final position (68–75). He
suggests the position of the final verb stands over against the first verb
in the verse, in effect "syntactically [defining] the parameters of the
poetic line" (69).

2:5   וַאֲנִי אָמַרְתִּי נִגְרַשְׁתִּי מִנֶּגֶד עֵינֶיךָ
אַךְ אוֹסִיף לְהַבִּיט אֶל־הֵיכַל קָדְשֶׁךָ:

וַאֲנִי אָמַרְתִּי. Expository discourse—off-the-line. Embedded oral
narrative continues. Within narrative discourse X + *qatal* is a form of
topicalization.

וַאֲנִי. The *waw* copulative before a non-verb constituent has a disjunctive role. Topicalization is used when there is a shift in participants (or scenes).

אָמַרְתִּי. Qal *qatal* 1 c s. On the use of אָמַר as a discourse switch cue, see 1:6.

נִגְרַשְׁתִּי מִנֶּגֶד עֵינֶיךָ. Expository discourse—off-the-line. The verb אָמַר signals that within the embedded oral narrative discourse (vv 3-4) another direct speech discourse will appear—a brief expository discourse in verse 5 appears embedded within the larger oral narrative discourse (which is embedded within the larger expository discourse of the entire poem).

נִגְרַשְׁתִּי. Niphal *qatal* 1 c s. A stative *qatal* verb expresses a state of affairs or a condition. Since a stative verb cannot actually express a singular, completed event, it necessarily carries a certain durative sense with it (termed the "persistent [present] perfective" by Waltke and O'Connor [487]). Further, when a stative *qatal* verb appears in dialogue, a present tense translation may better capture the durative sense.

מִנֶּגֶד. The complex preposition functions spatially, indicating the place from where an action is undertaken. As an adjunct to the verb, the prepositional phrase stands as an adverbial modifier.

עֵינֶיךָ. Object of preposition. Possessive pronoun.

אַךְ אוֹסִיף לְהַבִּיט אֶל־הֵיכַל קָדְשֶׁךָ. Expository discourse—off-the-line. In expository discourse, a *yiqtol* may appear in a clause that possesses a present time reference. The use of the clause initial *qatal* in the preceding clause provides such a reference.

אַךְ. The critical note in BHS proposes reading אֵיךְ in place of אַךְ. In Theodotion (θ´), the text reads πῶς, "how," and a number of translations and commentaries have sided with the reading in Theodotion. In support of such a reading, Wolff concludes that a question is "more probable than an expression of tenacious defiance or longing" at this point in the poem of Jonah (179). Yet given that the interrogative appears in only one textual tradition, the proposal must be abandoned and the MT retained. Landes retains the particle אַךְ, concluding that given the context of the poem, Jonah had no other recourse than to "resolve to turn to Yahweh in prayer" (22). The adverb may best be understood as a focus particle that is meant to place a limitation "with respect to the content of an expression directly preceding it," i.e., "nevertheless" (MNK, 313).

אוֹסִיף. Hiphil *yiqtol* 1 c s from יָסַף. Although present action is typically expressed through participles, a *yiqtol* may be employed to indicate the present tense when the action is considered "present continuous" (termed the "progressive non-perfective form" by Waltke and O'Connor [505]).

לְהַבִּיט. Hiphil inf constr from נָבַט. The Hiphil form of יָסַף typically requires an infinitive as a complement to the main verb.

אֶל־הֵיכַל קׇדְשֶׁךָ. The preposition is understood locationally, with the prepositional phrase functioning as an adjunct to the verb. The function of the second person pronominal suffix deserves mention. As van der Merwe, Naudé, and Kroeze explain, "A pronominal suffix that belongs to the *status constructus* 'jumps' to the next possible position" (196). Yet in translating the entire construct phrase, the suffix must be translated as part of the construct noun [*status constructus*]. In addition, while the construct noun can fulfill any syntactic function, the absolute noun can only be an adjectival qualification of the construct noun. Thus, although the text literally reads "to the temple of your holiness," the construction is better translated as "to your holy temple."

2:6   אֲפָפוּנִי מַיִם עַד־נֶפֶשׁ תְּהוֹם יְסֹבְבֵנִי
        סוּף חָבוּשׁ לְרֹאשִׁי׃

אֲפָפוּנִי מַיִם עַד־נֶפֶשׁ. Expository discourse—off-the-line. Following the direct speech in verse 5, the psalm returns to embedded oral narrative discourse.

אֲפָפוּנִי. Qal *qatal* 3 c p + 1 c s suffix. On the implications of the *qatal* as clause initial, see 2:3. The verb is rare, occurring only in poetic texts (2 Sam 22:5; Pss 18:5; 40:13; 116:3).

מַיִם. Subject of אֲפָפוּנִי.

עַד־נֶפֶשׁ. The preposition is understood locationally, with the prepositional phrase functioning as an adjunct to the verb.

תְּהוֹם יְסֹבְבֵנִי. Expository discourse—off-the-line. Continuation of embedded oral narrative discourse.

תְּהוֹם. Fronted subject of יְסֹבְבֵנִי.

יְסֹבְבֵנִי. Polel *yiqtol* 3 m s + 1 c s suffix. On the *yiqtol* as an "incipient past non-perfective," see 2:4.

סוּף חָבוּשׁ לְרֹאשִׁי. Expository discourse—off-the-line. Within embedded oral narrative discourse, the participles provide background information. Thus the clause does not move the narrative forward, it simply enhances the image being presented through providing additional information.

סוּף. Elsewhere in the Hebrew Bible, סוּף refers to either the reeds that grow in Egyptian waters or the body of water known as the יַם סוּף. The choice of סוּף in this context appears somewhat strange given the rather narrow semantic range of the word. The word may have been selected for rhetorical reasons. The repetition of the ו in חָבוּשׁ סוּף is an example of assonance. More difficult to confirm is the possibility that the author has chosen a term that generates a sense of ambiguity, similar to the use of the Polel form סָבַב in 2:4 and 2:6a. סוּף is often understood as a place of deliverance (Exod 2:3; Exod 15:4). The author may have adopted an unusual use of סוּף in order to highlight the deliverance announced in 2:7.

חָבוּשׁ. Qal pass ptc. The participle is understood as a predicate adjective. Waltke and O'Connor suggest that the passive participle may possess an "inchoative state," that is, the participle focuses on the subject coming into some form of modified state (620).

לְרֹאשִׁי. The preposition has a spatial sense. The verb חָבַשׁ is frequently followed by prepositional phrases (using בְּ, לְ, and עַל). Possessive pronoun.

$$
\begin{array}{r}
\text{לְקִצְבֵי הָרִים} \qquad \text{2:7} \\
\text{יָרַדְתִּי הָאָרֶץ בְּרִחֶיהָ בַעֲדִי לְעוֹלָם} \\
\text{וַתַּעַל מִשַּׁחַת חַיַּי יהוה אֱלֹהָי:}
\end{array}
$$

לְקִצְבֵי הָרִים יָרַדְתִּי. Expository discourse—off-the-line. Following both the LXX and the Latin, Wolff has suggested that לְקִצְבֵי הָרִים be read with the final clause in 2:6, סוֹף חָבוּשׁ לְרֹאשִׁי, thus preserving a five stress line (127). While the NRSV renders the verset similarly (linking 7a with 6c), both the NAS and the NIV retain the division in the MT. Such a division in the line is a poetic feature referred to as "enjambment." This is "present when a sentence or a clause does not end when the colon ends but runs over into the next colon" (Watson, 333). Thus verse 6c has run over into the next colon and verse 7a appears in an effort to retain the structure of the line. The result is an X + *qatal* structure in verse 7a. In embedded narrative discourse, the X + *qatal* indicates topicalization. In fronting לְקִצְבֵי הָרִים, the focus has shifted to the location from which Jonah will be "brought up."

לְקִצְבֵי הָרִים. The preposition is understood locationally, with the prepositional phrase functioning as an adjunct to the verb. BHS suggests reading לְקַצְוֵי for לְקִצְבֵי, thus rendering the phrase "the ends of the mountains." Yet such a proposal fails to recognize the cosmological imagery present in the immediate context of the poem (הָאָרֶץ; תְּהוֹם) and moreover, the cosmological imagery inherent in the phrase itself. For example, קִצְבֵי הָרִים appears Sir 16:19 where it stands parallel to "the foundations of the world."

יָרַדְתִּי. Qal *qatal* 1 c s.

הָאָרֶץ בְּרִחֶיהָ בַעֲדִי לְעוֹלָם. Expository discourse—off-the-line. Within embedded oral narrative discourse, verbless clauses provide "scene setting" information—the clause is meant to indicate the plight of Jonah.

הָאָרֶץ. Subject of verbless clause.

בְּרִחֶיהָ. The noun stands in apposition to **הָאָרֶץ**, with the second term qualifying the head. Together they function as the subject of the verbless clause. In addition to the rendering above, one may also render an appositional phrase in a manner similar to a construct phrase, i.e., "the bars of Sheol" (WO, 229; MNK, 228–29).

בַעֲדִי. The preposition indicates localization and frequently follows verbs that refer to a process of closure (MNK, 283). Although the clause is verbless, the association of the preposition with such verbs elsewhere contributes to a similar notion in this context. The absence of the expected verb may be attributed to either ellipsis, or simply the terseness of language that characterizes Hebrew poetry (cf. Berlin).

לְעוֹלָם. Independent temporal adverb.

וַתַּעַל מִשַּׁחַת חַיַּי יְהוָה אֱלֹהָי. Expository discourse—off-the-line. Within embedded oral narrative discourse, a *wayyiqtol* resumes the progression of the narrative flow (interrupted by the X + *qatal* and verbless clauses).

וַתַּעַל. Hiphil *wayyiqtol* 2 m s from **עָלָה**.

מִשַּׁחַת. Spatial sense of the preposition. The prepositional phrase operates as an adjunct to the verb.

חַיַּי. Direct object of **וַתַּעַל**. Possessive pronoun.

יְהוָה אֱלֹהָי. Vocative. Possessive pronoun. Vocatives often appear in direct speech discourse and stand in apposition to a second person pronoun or the "built-in" subject of the verb.

בְּהִתְעַטֵּף עָלַי֙ נַפְשִׁי֙ אֶת־יְהוָה זָכָ֑רְתִּי   2:8
וַתָּב֤וֹא אֵלֶ֙יךָ֙ תְּפִלָּתִ֔י אֶל־הֵיכַ֖ל קָדְשֶֽׁךָ׃

בְּהִתְעַטֵּף עָלַי נַפְשִׁי. Expository discourse—off-the-line. The temporal infinitive clause is subordinate to the main clause in the line.

בְּהִתְעַטֵּף. Prep + Hith inf constr. Temporal infinitive clause. בְּ + an infinitive construct tends to denote the temporal proximity of one event to another (WO, 604).

עָלַי. עַל is understood reflexively. Waltke and O'Connor note that in circumstances where "the subject feels the pathos 'upon' himself, or herself, the [עַל] phrase is reflexive" (217). See Psalm 143:4 for a similar use of the preposition. Objective pronoun.

נַפְשִׁי. Subject of infinitive constr. Possessive pronoun.

אֶת־יְהוָה זָכָרְתִּי. Expository discourse—off-the-line. On the X + *qatal* construction in embedded narrative, see 2:7.

אֶת־יְהוָה. Fronted direct object of verb.

זָכָרְתִּי. Qal *qatal* 1 c s.

וַתָּבוֹא אֵלֶיךָ תְּפִלָּתִי אֶל־הֵיכַל קָדְשֶׁךָ. Expository discourse—off-the-line. The *wayyiqtol* verb form indicates the continuance of the embedded oral narrative, with an unmarked order.

וַתָּבוֹא. Qal *wayyiqtol* 3 f s.

אֵלֶיךָ. The prepositional phrase functions as a complement to the verb, with the preposition marking the indirect object.

תְּפִלָּתִי. Subject of וַתָּבוֹא.

אֶל־הֵיכַל קָדְשֶׁךָ. See 2:5.

מְשַׁמְּרִים הַבְלֵי־שָׁוְא   חַסְדָּם יַעֲזֹבוּ:   2:9

Expository discourse—off-the-line. The line may be more properly understood as a monocolon (Watson, 168–77). The monocolon may serve a variety of functions, but the monocolon in verse 9 functions as a climactic monocolon, highlighting the contrast between the מְשַׁמְּרִים הַבְלֵי־שָׁוְא in verse 9 and the poet in verse 10. Within expository discourse, the *yiqtol* form can suggest present time reference.

מְשַׁמְּרִים. Piel ptc m p. Relative use of the participle (WO, 621). Participial phrases often appear in a *casus pendens* construction (JM, 588).

הַבְלֵי־שָׁוְא. The use of two substantives with near synonymous meanings in a construct relationship can be used to express a superlative (JM, 525). The phrase הַבְלֵי־שָׁוְא is no doubt understood as referring to idols (cf. Deut 32:21 where הֶבֶל appears parallel to לֹא־אֵל), but the superlative force of the construction heightens the intensity of claim. The NRSV fails to capture the intensity with "vain idols." Wolff comes closer with his somewhat enigmatic rendering, "unfounded Nothingness."

חַסְדָּם. Direct object of יַעֲזֹבוּ. Possessive use of pronoun. The precise meaning of the noun חֶסֶד in this line has generated a number of proposals. The prevailing opinion is that חֶסֶד should be understood as referring metonymically to God, thus creating a comparison between that which they "keep" or "worship" (הַבְלֵי־שָׁוְא) and that which they forsake (חֶסֶד, i.e., Yahweh). See Walsh. Alternatively, the noun could refer to the חֶסֶד of those whom the poet calls מְשַׁמְּרִים הַבְלֵי־שָׁוְא. Taken as such, the line suggests that those who worship worthless objects demonstrate their disregard of covenantal commitments (Kamp, 142 n. 76; Barré, 241). Such as reading contributes to the notion of verse 9 as a climactic monocolon. The disregard of covenant commitments by those in verse 9 is set in contrast to the emphatic declaration of Jonah and his commitments.

יַעֲזֹבוּ. Qal *yiqtol* 3 m p.

> 2:10 וַאֲנִי בְּקוֹל תּוֹדָה אֶזְבְּחָה־לָּךְ
> אֲשֶׁר נָדַרְתִּי אֲשַׁלֵּמָה יְשׁוּעָתָה לַיהוָה:

וַאֲנִי בְּקוֹל תּוֹדָה אֶזְבְּחָה־לָּךְ. Expository discourse—off-the-line. The clause is doubly fronted, marking not only the exclusive role of a particular discourse active entity, but also marking a particular quality of the discourse active event as well. As with verse 9, the doubly fronted *yiqtol* continues the narrative in the present tense, while also paralleling in construction the monocolon in verse 9.

וַאֲנִי. See 2:5.

בְּקוֹל תּוֹדָה. Instrumental sense of the preposition (*beth instrumenti*). The absolute noun functions attributively in the construct phrase.

אֶזְבְּחָה. Piel *yiqtol* 1 c s + coh *he*. Although difficult to capture in translation, the cohortative is meant to indicate the speaker's resolve, which stands in contrast to the lack of resolve of the מְשַׁמְּרִים הַבְלֵי־שָׁוְא.

לָּךְ. The prepositional phrase functions as a complement to the verb, with the preposition marking the indirect object. Objective pronoun.

אֲשֶׁר נָדַרְתִּי אֲשַׁלֵּמָה. Expository discourse—off-the-line.

אֲשֶׁר. Introduces an object clause.

נָדַרְתִּי. Qal *qatal* 1 c s. The *qatal* in a dependent clause provides information that is background to the main clause, and should be rendered in English as a present perfect ("have vowed").

אֲשַׁלֵּמָה. Qal *yiqtol* 1 c s + coh *he*. On the cohortative, see above.

יְשׁוּעָתָה לַיהוָה. Expository discourse—mainline. The final clause in the poem is actually the only clause in which there is a mainline verbal form for expository discourse—a verbless clause. The previous clauses have all been off-the-line forms that have provided background information to the central claim of the poem. In essence, the entire poem has been constructed as an argument which culminates with the primary thesis (Rocine, 319) being presented in verse 10bβ.

יְשׁוּעָ֫תָה. The lexical form for the feminine noun is יְשׁוּעָה, but it is one of a number of feminine nouns that frequently take תָה ָ- as an ending, particularly in poetic texts (GKC, 251; cf. Ps 3:3).

לַיהוָה. The lack of agreement in definiteness between the two nouns requires the use of a periphrastic construction to indicate possession (MNK, 197; WO, 157).

Jonah 2:11

[11]And then the LORD spoke to the fish and the fish vomited Jonah onto the dry land.

2:11 וַיֹּ֤אמֶר יְהוָה֙ לַדָּ֔ג וַיָּקֵ֥א אֶת־יוֹנָ֖ה אֶל־הַיַּבָּשָֽׁה׃

וַיֹּ֤אמֶר יְהוָה֙ לַדָּ֔ג. Narrative discourse—mainline. The *wayyiqtol* serves as a discourse switch cue, indicating the move from expository to narrative discourse.

וַיֹּ֤אמֶר. Qal *wayyiqtol* 3 m s. Previous uses of the verb אָמַר have been followed by direct speech. In 2:11, there is no direct speech to follow, but the speech report may best be understood as diegetic summary (Miller, 137). In such speech reports, the reported quotation is not provided, but the "perlocutionary effect of the quotation is reported in the following clause" (138). Thus, although the content and purpose of the speech event may be inferred from the subsequent events, the precise words cannot be recovered. Miller contends that diegetic summaries are narrative techniques meant to condense the command and the execution of the command (139).

יְהוָה. Subject of וַיֹּאמֶר.

לַדָּג. The prepositional phrase functions as a complement to the verb, marking out the indirect object.

וַיָּקֵא אֶת־יוֹנָה אֶל־הַיַּבָּשָׁה. Narrative discourse—mainline.

וַיָּקֵא. Qal *wayyiqtol* 3 m s from קיא.

אֶת־יוֹנָה. Direct object of וַיָּקֵא.

אֶל־הַיַּבָּשָׁה. See 1:13.

Jonah 3:1-4

[1]Now the word of the LORD came to Jonah a second time, [2]"Set out for Nineveh, the great city, and announce to it the proclamation that I am giving to you." [3]And then Jonah set out and went to Nineveh according to the word of the LORD. Nineveh was a great city belonging to God, a journey of three days. [4]And then Jonah proceeded to go into the city a journey of one day. And then he cried out and said, "Yet forty days and Nineveh is going to be overturned."

3:1   וַיְהִי דְבַר־יְהוָה אֶל־יוֹנָה שֵׁנִית לֵאמֹר:

Narrative discourse—mainline. The third chapter of Jonah opens with a construction almost identical to that found in the first chapter. In the first chapter however, it was noted that the verb appeared to deviate from conventional use. The third chapter employs the verb וַיְהִי in a manner more consistent with traditional usage of the form. Often the verb signals that a new scene is to be linked with a preceding one. The use of the adjective שֵׁנִית serves to confirm such linkage with earlier events.

וַיְהִי. See 1:1.

דְבַר־יְהוָה. See 1:1

אֶל־יוֹנָה. See 1:1.

שֵׁנִית. The patronym of the prophet mentioned in 1:1 has been replaced with feminine ordinal adjective. Limburg suggests that שֵׁנִית implies "a repetition of the word that came the first time" (1993, 75). The use of the adjective שֵׁנִית however, does not necessarily suggest that the same message came to Jonah, only that "the word of the Lord" came to Jonah a second time (See Sasson, 225–26). The shift in prepositions in 3:2 (from עַל to אֶל) may raise addition questions about the nature of this message (see below).

לֵאמֹר. See 1:1. Note that the verb serves as a discourse switch cue.

3:2   קוּם לֵךְ אֶל־נִינְוֵה הָעִיר הַגְּדוֹלָה וּקְרָא אֵלֶיהָ אֶת־
       הַקְּרִיאָה אֲשֶׁר אָנֹכִי דֹּבֵר אֵלֶיךָ:

קוּם לֵךְ אֶל־נִינְוֵה הָעִיר הַגְּדוֹלָה. Embedded hortatory discourse—mainline. See 1:2.

קוּם. See 1.2.

לֵךְ. See 1:2.

אֶל־נִינְוֵה. See 1:2

הָעִיר הַגְּדוֹלָה. See 1:2.

וּקְרָא אֵלֶיהָ אֶת־הַקְּרִיאָה. Embedded hortatory discourse—mainline.

וּקְרָא. *Waw* cop + Qal impv 2 m s. The vocabulary in 3:2 duplicates that of 1:2 up to the point of the preposition following קְרָא. In 1:2, the verb קְרָא was followed by the preposition עַל, and translated as "cry out against." Although the preposition אֶל may mark an ethical dative of interest, advantage or disadvantage (WO, 193) and thus translated as "against" (cf. Num 32:14), such is not the case when the preposition is coupled with the verb קְרָא (contra Snaith who reads the two as synonymous [31]). The phrase קָרָא אֶל occurs 52 times in the Hebrew Bible, with the preposition functioning as a adjunct to the verb, marking out the recipient of the speech (AC, 99). On the distinction between 1:2 and 3:2, see also Sasson, 72–75.

The pointing of the conjunction merits attention. The *waw* copulative is pointed both as a *šûreq* and a *ḥîreq*. While either is possible, both are not. The BHS note explains that the Leningrad text offers two readings: וּקְרָא and וְקְרָא. The note also suggests that many other manuscript editions include וּקְרָא. Either form would be rendered similarly in translation.

אֵלֶיהָ. The prepositional phrase functions as a complement to the verb, marking out the goal of the saying process. Objective pronoun.

אֶת־הַקְּרִיאָה. The object is an internal adjunct, but with no additional semantic value (see 1:16). The term is a *hapex legomenon* (but occurs with regularity in the rabbinic literature [Sasson, 226]). The narrator's preference for internal adjuncts may explain its inclusion.

אֲשֶׁר אָנֹכִי דֹּבֵר אֵלֶיךָ. Embedded hortatory discourse—off-the-line. The relative clause offers background information related to the mainline of the clause. In particular, the relative clause offers information related to the nature of הַקְּרִיאָה. Although the narrator does not specify the precise content of the message, the point is clear that הַקְּרִיאָה is given to Jonah by God.

אֲשֶׁר. Rel pronoun. The antecedent to the relative pronoun is הַקְּרִיאָה, and operates as the object of the relative clause.

אָנֹכִי דֹּבֵר. 1 c s pronoun – Qal act ptc. The noun and the participle are in unmarked word order. Although דָּבַר occurs primarily in the Piel, it does occur as a participle in the Qal (perhaps once as an infinitive, BDB, 180). The Qal participle form of דָּבַר is joined with the preposition אֶל six other times in the Hebrew Bible (Gen 16:13; Exod 6:29; Jer 38:20; 40:16; Job 2:13; Dan 10:11). The construction דָּבַר אֶל may refer to instructions that will be given (Exod 6:29; Dan

10:11) as well as to information already communicated (Jer 48:20). It should be noted however that when the phrase appears as a statement from God or a divine being (Exod 6:29; Dan 10:11), it appears to refer to information that will be communicated.

אֵלֶיךָ. The prepositional phrase functions as a complement to the verb, marking out the goal of the saying process. Objective pronoun.

3:3 וַיָּקָם יוֹנָה וַיֵּלֶךְ אֶל־נִינְוֶה כִּדְבַר יְהוָה וְנִינְוֶה הָיְתָה
עִיר־גְּדוֹלָה לֵאלֹהִים מַהֲלַךְ שְׁלֹשֶׁת יָמִים:

וַיָּקָם יוֹנָה. Narrative discourse—mainline. The *wayyiqtol* verb serves as a discourse switch cue, shifting the discourse from embedded hortatory discourse to narrative discourse.

וַיָּקָם. Qal *wayyiqtol* 3 m s from קוּם.

יוֹנָה. Subject of וַיָּקָם.

וַיֵּלֶךְ אֶל־נִינְוֶה כִּדְבַר יְהוָה. Narrative discourse—mainline.

וַיֵּלֶךְ. Qal *wayyiqtol* 3 m s from הָלַךְ. This clause introduces the first major departure from the outline of events in chapter 1. In 1:3, a Qal infinitive construct followed the first two words in the phrase: וַיָּקָם יוֹנָה לִבְרֹחַ. In 3:3, however, the narrative departs from the construction in 1:3 by reverting to a *wayyiqtol*, thus continuing the flow of the narrative in chapter 3.

אֶל־נִינְוֶה. The prepositional phrase functions as a complement to the verb, marking out the goal of the movement (MNK, 244).

כִּדְבַר יְהוָה. Unlike the other inseparable prepositions, the preposition כְּ has no spatial sense. The primary function of the preposition is to note comparison and correspondence (between the action of Jonah [וַיָּקָם יוֹנָה וַיֵּלֶךְ אֶל־נִינְוֶה] and the word of Yahweh). The prepositional phrase, כִּדְבַר יְהוָה, may be understood as an oracle fulfillment formula, thus fulfilling the oracle issued in 3:1.

וְנִינְוֵה הָיְתָה עִיר־גְּדוֹלָה לֵאלֹהִים. Narrative discourse—off-the-line. The X + *qatal* construction signals topicalization, thus indicating a shift in focus in the middle of the discourse. The narrative provides background information related to the fronted element, נִינְוֵה. More particularly, however, the X + הָיָה construction is "as grammatically bold-faced as a statement of fact can get" (Rocine, 338), thus serving to mark a high point in the text (Dawson, 159). Thus the clause may signal not only a shift in focus, but also a major contribution to the work as a whole.

וְנִינְוֵה. Fronted noun serves as subject of הָיְתָה. A *waw* copulative may be used to join clauses in which "the content of the clause with ו refers to background information necessary for understanding the other [clause] better" (MNK, 299). Frequently such a use will be translated as "now."

הָיְתָה. Qal *qatal* 3 f s from הָיָה.

עִיר־גְּדוֹלָה. The noun phrase serves as a predicate complement. On the types of complements of הָיָה, see Sinclair, 61–75.

לֵאלֹהִים. The relationship between לֵאלֹהִים and עִיר־גְּדוֹלָה has generated considerable discussion, with at least three options prevailing. The first would be to understand the use of the divine name idiomatically, or more specifically, adjectively. In this case, the divine name operates as a type of superlative, rendering the phrase "an exceedingly great city." Such a use of the divine name is not altogether unusual in the Hebrew Bible (cf. 1 Sam 14:15; Gen 23:6). To provide additional support for this option, commentators will turn to archaeological and historical data, citing the sheer enormity of the city, hence justifying such a translation (Wolff, 148; Allen, 221–22). Although such a position is frequently adopted (WO, 268; JPS; NRSV; NIV), Sasson notes that the construction in Jonah does not follow the use of the divine name for the superlative elsewhere in the canon. In other locations, the divine name immediately follows the noun being modified without interruption.

A second possibility would be to render the phrase literally, "a great city to the gods," or "a large city to God." In chapter 1, the meaning of אֱלֹהִים proved ambiguous at points, but at this point in the narrative, the author has set aside such ambiguity. To return to an ambiguous meaning of אֱלֹהִים, or worse yet, one that speaks of the gods of Assyria would seem counter productive to the plot of the narrative.

A final option would be to render the phrase "a great city belonging to God." In this case, the phrase is understood as a circumlocution in which the preposition introduces a noun function with a genitive sense (GKC, 419–20). Although such a sense is typically expressed with the use of a simple construct chain in Hebrew, the disparity in definiteness between עִיר־גְּדוֹלָה and אֱלֹהִים warrants consideration of a different construction (the use of אֱלֹהִים in 3:5 would confirm the narrator's use of אֱלֹהִים as definite). The preposition לְ may be inserted to prevent "a *nomen regens* being determined by a following determinate noun" (GKC, 419). For example, the phrase בֶּן־יִשַׁי would be rendered "*the* son of Jesse" due to the definiteness of the absolute noun. But if one wanted to render the phrase "*a* son of Jesse," a preposition would have to be inserted, בֵּן לְיִשַׁי. Since Nineveh is not *the* great city belonging to God, but a great city belonging to God, a circumlocution is necessary.

In addition, an affirmation that Nineveh *belongs* to God plays into the irony of the book, invoking the universal compassion of Israel's God despite the narcissism implicit in the actions of Jonah. Further, such a reading corresponds with the notion that the construction of the clause is "grammatically bold-faced." Such a reading also appears to foreshadow the final proclamation of God in 4:10-11.

מַהֲלַךְ שְׁלֹשֶׁת יָמִים. The phrase stands as an elliptical clause. Frequently, an elliptical clause appears when the antecedents (וְנִינְוֵה הָיְתָה) are clear from the context (AC, 192). The gender of שְׁלֹשֶׁת (feminine) is the expected form when accompanied by a masculine plural noun.

3:4 וַיָּ֤חֶל יוֹנָה֙ לָב֣וֹא בָעִ֔יר מַהֲלַ֖ךְ י֣וֹם אֶחָ֑ד וַיִּקְרָא֙
וַיֹּאמַ֔ר ע֚וֹד אַרְבָּעִ֣ים י֔וֹם וְנִֽינְוֵ֖ה נֶהְפָּֽכֶת׃

וַיָּ֤חֶל יוֹנָה לָבוֹא בָעִיר מַהֲלַךְ יוֹם אֶחָד. Narrative discourse—mainline. The presence of a *wayyiqtol* signals a shift back
to the mainline of the narrative. The last clause on the mainline,
וַיֵּ֙לֶךְ֙ אֶל־נִֽינְוֵ֔ה כִּדְבַ֖ר יְהוָ֑ה, was "interrupted" by the X + *qatal*
clause. With the opening clause in 3:4, the narrative returns to the
events related to יוֹנָה.

וַיָּחֶל. Hiph *wayyiqtol* 3 m s from חָלַל (III). In the Niphal, Piel, and
Pual, חָלַל consistently means "to pollute, defile, or profane." In the
Hiphil, חָלַל conveys the meaning of polluting or profaning in only
two instances (Num 30:3; Ezek 39:7). In the remaining instances,
however, the verb refers to the inception of an event. In such cases,
חָלַל is followed by an infinitive construct coupled with a לְ.

יוֹנָה. Subject of וַיָּחֶל.

לָבוֹא. Prep + Qal inf constr. The infinitive serves as a complement
to וַיָּחֶל.

בָעִיר. When used with verbs of movement, the preposition is
understood in a spatial sense, with particular focus on the movement
in or into a domain (WO, 196).

מַהֲלַךְ יוֹם אֶחָד. The construct phrase expresses an adverbial
relationship, with the construct noun indicating the entity, while the
absolute noun notes the duration of time (MNK, 199).

וַיִּקְרָא. Narrative discourse—mainline. Qal *wayyiqtol* 3 m s. On the
use of the multiple-verb frame (קָרָא + אָמַר) as a quotative frame,
see 1:14.

וַיֹּאמַר. Narrative discourse—mainline. Qal *wayyiqtol* 3 m s.

ע֚וֹד אַרְבָּעִים יוֹם וְנִינְוֵה נֶהְפָּכֶת. Expository discourse—mainline. Although verbless clauses typically constitute the mainline of expository speech, Rocine has suggested clauses with verbal participles are of equally high ranking (318).

עוֹד. The adverb עוֹד is understood as an independent temporal adverb with the primary purpose of noting the time of the action to which the verb refers (WO, 657; MNK, 308).

אַרְבָּעִים יוֹם. The phrase עוֹד אַרְבָּעִים יוֹם is understood as an example of *casus pendens*, given that it stands outside the clausal predication. The subsequent *waw* separates it from the remainder of the clause, but the *casus pendens* does retain a pragmatic function, that of providing a temporal framework for what follows (MNK, 339).

Typically when the value of the numeral is greater than one (1) the noun will appear in the plural. Frequently, however, nouns may be used collectively with numerals (MNK, 268).

וְנִינְוֵה. Fronted subject of נֶהְפָּכֶת.

נֶהְפָּכֶת. Niph ptc f s. Sasson attempts to translate the verb duratively, "and Nineveh overturns," but the verb seems more likely to be understood as indicating imminent action, also known as a *futurum instans* participle. Waltke and O'Connor suggest that the notion of "certainty" with "immanency" is understood semantically and may be connoted by the English "I am going to. . ." (627). Arnold and Choi suggest that the Old Testament prophets make frequent use of the future predicate participle for rhetorical effect (81).

The somewhat ambiguous meaning of הָפַךְ in 3:4 is central to the plot of Jonah. In the Qal, the verb frequently describes the turning, or overturning, of a city as a result of judgment. The verb appears in association with the overturning of Sodom and Gomorrah. A similar use, albeit one couched in eschatological imagery, appears in Haggai's description of God overturning the armies and thrones of the earth's kingdoms (2:21-22). In the Niphal, however, the verb frequently carries the connotation of "turning" but frequently in the sense of changing or turning back, as well as that of deliverance (cf. Exod 14:5; 1 Sam

10:6; Isa 60:5; 63:10; Jer 2:21; 31:13; Ps 66:6). In Hosea 11:8, the heart of God is "overturned" or "changed." In other places, the Niphal form still retains the notion of physical destruction associated with the Qal form (cf. Josh 8:20). The ambiguity of Jonah's announcement accords well with the narrator's ironic tone.

Jonah 3:5-9

⁵Then the men of Nineveh believed in God. They proclaimed a fast and put on sackcloth, from the greatest of them to the least. ⁶Then the word reached the King of Nineveh, and he arose from his throne and took off his robe which was upon him and he covered himself in sackcloth and sat in ashes. ⁷Then he made a proclamation in Nineveh based on the judgment of the king and his nobles: "Humans and beasts—herd or flock—shall not taste anything. Let them not graze nor drink water. ⁸Let the human beings and animals cover themselves in sackcloth and cry mightily to God. Let each turn from his evil way and from the violence which is on their hands. ⁹Who knows? God may turn back and relent. He may turn from his anger so that we do not perish."

3:5　וַיַּאֲמִ֤ינוּ אַנְשֵׁ֣י נִֽינְוֵה֙ בֵּֽאלֹהִ֔ים וַיִּקְרְאוּ־צוֹם֙ וַיִּלְבְּשׁ֣וּ
שַׂקִּ֔ים מִגְּדוֹלָ֖ם וְעַד־קְטַנָּֽם׃

וַיַּאֲמִינוּ אַנְשֵׁי נִֽינְוֵה בֵּאלֹהִים. Narrative discourse—mainline.

וַיַּאֲמִינוּ. Hiph *wayyiqtol* 3 m p. In the Hiphil, אָמַן means "to trust" or "to believe." When the verb is followed by the inseparable preposition בְּ, the verb means "to trust in" or "to have faith in" (BDB, 53). Although בְּ frequently connotes a "spatial" sense ("in"), the preposition marks the object of verbs of emotion, especially אָמַן. The use of the verb in the Hiphil followed by the בְּ conjoined to יְהוָה appears with some regularity in the Hebrew Bible (Gen 15:6; Exod 14:31; Num

14:11; 20:12; Deut 1:32; 2 Kgs 17:14; 2 Chr 20:20). The same construction with אֱלֹהִים in place of the divine name appears only here and in Psalm 78:22 (explained by its location in the Elohistic Psalter).

אַנְשֵׁי נִינְוֵה. The construct relationship expresses possession (frequently termed a "possessive genitive" [WO, 145]).

בֵאלֹהִים. See above for use of preposition with the verb אָמַן.

וַיִּקְרְאוּ־צוֹם. Narrative discourse—mainline.

וַיִּקְרְאוּ. Qal *wayyiqtol* 3 m p. In prior instances in the book, the verb קָרָא has appeared as part of a quotative frame (typically in association with אָמַר). This is the first non-quotative use of the verb. On the function of diegetic summaries, see 2:11.

צוֹם. Direct object of וַיִּקְרְאוּ. Although the noun form may appear as an internal adjunct when coupled with the verb צוּם, it frequently appears as the object of the verb קָרָא (1 Kgs 21:9, 12; 2 Chr 20:3; Ezek 8:21; Jer 36:9).

וַיִּלְבְּשׁוּ שַׂקִּים מִגְּדוֹלָם וְעַד־קְטַנָּם. Narrative discourse—mainline.

וַיִּלְבְּשׁוּ. Qal *wayyiqtol* 3 m p.

שַׂקִּים. Direct object of וַיִּלְבְּשׁוּ.

מִגְּדוֹלָם וְעַד־קְטַנָּם. Both adjectives (גָּדוֹל and קָטֹן) are used substantively, with the preposition מִן expressing the superlative. The entire phrase מִגְּדוֹלָם וְעַד־קְטַנָּם is a merismus, but within the context of the present sentence, the phrase also appears as a type of pleonasm (Trible, 1994, 181). Although the earlier phrase אַנְשֵׁי נִינְוֵה underscores the comprehensive nature of the response, the subsequent phrase מִגְּדוֹלָם וְעַד־קְטַנָּם highlights the inclusivity of the response, "from the greatest to the least of them." The second phrase, while grammatically unnecessary (hence pleonastic), nonetheless adds emphasis and depth to the language.

3:6 וַיִּגַּע הַדָּבָר אֶל־מֶלֶךְ נִינְוֵה וַיָּקָם מִכִּסְאוֹ וַיַּעֲבֵר
אַדַּרְתּוֹ מֵעָלָיו וַיְכַס שַׂק וַיֵּשֶׁב עַל־הָאֵפֶר:

וַיִּגַּע הַדָּבָר אֶל־מֶלֶךְ נִינְוֵה. Narrative discourse—mainline.

וַיִּגַּע. Qal *wayyiqtol* 3 m s from נָגַע. Although the verbal root נָגַע
connotes the meaning of "to touch" or "to strike," the use of the root
followed by the preposition אֶל often results in a meaning similar "to
come" or "to reach" (BDB, 618). As Sasson notes, the term is tactile,
not emotional. Had the narrator intended to indicate that the דָּבָר had
"touched" the king, the preposition employed with נָגַע would have
been בְּ (on the use of בְּ with verbs of emotion, see 3:5). Wolff (151)
and Stuart (484) fail to observe this distinction and unfortunately
provide an "emotional" sense to the term, rendering it as "touch."

הַדָּבָר. Because the noun דָּבָר can be translated as "speech,"
"word," or "event," along with a host of other possible meanings, the
precise meaning or referent may prove difficult to assess (on the notion
of lexical ambiguity, see WO, 223). There are at least three options as
to the precise referent of the term. הַדָּבָר could refer to the speech of
Jonah (עוֹד אַרְבָּעִים יוֹם וְנִינְוֵה נֶהְפָּכֶת), although Jonah's words are
referred to as a proclamation (הַקְּרִיאָה) in 3:2. The second option,
with obvious connections to the first is that throughout the book
דָּבָר has been coupled with יְהוָה (1:1; 3:1, 3). Hence הַדָּבָר could
be referring to the דְּבַר־יְהוָה, with the absence of the divine name
being attributed to ellipsis. The third option is that הַדָּבָר refers to the
preceding events in the city, although Wolff (151) suggests that if that
were the intended subject, one would expect to find הַדְּבָרִים הָאֵלֶּה,
"these things" (cf. Gen 15:1; 1 Kgs 17:17; 21:1). The first option seems
preferable, given that דָּבָר is often employed to speak of the prophetic
word (Jer 18:18; Amos 3:1; Ezek 33:30).

אֶל־מֶלֶךְ נִינְוֵה. The prepositional phrase functions as a complement to a "prepositional verb" (MNK, 275).

וַיָּ֫קָם מִכִּסְא֑וֹ. Narrative discourse—mainline.

וַיָּ֫קָם. Qal *wayyiqtol* 3 m s from קוּם. In 1:2 and 3:2, קוּם operated as an auxiliary verb in conjunction with הָלַךְ and intended to convey volition. קוּם appears absent of הָלַךְ in the present verse, and no doubt references directional movement.

מִכִּסְא֑וֹ. The prepositional phrase operates as an adjunct to the verb. Spatial sense of the preposition. Possessive pronoun.

וַיַּעֲבֵ֥ר אַדַּרְתּ֖וֹ מֵעָלָ֑יו. Narrative discourse—mainline.

וַיַּעֲבֵ֥ר. Qal *wayyiqtol* 3 m s.

אַדַּרְתּ֖וֹ. Direct object of וַיַּעֲבֵ֥ר. Possessive pronoun.

מֵעָלָ֑יו. The prepositional phrase stands as an adjunct to the verb, and is understood locatively. Objective pronoun.

וַיְכַ֣ס שָׂ֔ק. Narrative discourse—mainline.

וַיְכַ֣ס. Piel *wayyiqtol* 3 m s from כָּסָה. The verb appears in apocopated form. The verb לָבַשׁ is the expected verb when שָׂק is the object of the verb. The narrator may have chosen the unusual verb for two reasons. First, כָּסָה creates a word play with the word for throne, כִּסֵּא. Second, and perhaps more subtle, the narrator may have also selected this term because it is frequently found in texts that speak of redemption—terms such as "transgression," "righteousness," "guilt," or "iniquity" (BDB, 491). The verb should be understood reflexively.

שָׂ֔ק. Direct object of the וַיְכַ֣ס. Elsewhere in the Hebrew Bible, when שָׂק appears as the object of the verb כָּסָה, the preposition בְּ is attached, hence the phrase, "he put *on* sackcloth" (2 Kgs 19:1, 2; Isa 37:1, 2; 1 Chr 21:16). שָׂק appears as the object of כָּסָה in two other locations, here and in 3:8. In both cases, however, the preposition is absent. To alleviate the awkwardness of the construction, the verbal form could be emended (BDB, 491). Yet as Sasson notes, the narrator appears to have a penchant for idiomatic language, particularly when it contributes to multiple layers of meaning.

וַיֵּ֖שֶׁב עַל־הָאֵֽפֶר. Narrative discourse—mainline.

וַיֵּ֖שֶׁב. Qal *wayyiqtol* 3 m s from יָשַׁב.

עַל־הָאֵֽפֶר. The preposition is understood locatively, with the prepositional phrase functioning as an adjunct to the verb.

> 3:7 וַיַּזְעֵ֗ק וַיֹּ֙אמֶר֙ בְּנִֽינְוֵ֔ה מִטַּ֧עַם הַמֶּ֛לֶךְ וּגְדֹלָ֖יו לֵאמֹ֑ר
> הָאָדָ֨ם וְהַבְּהֵמָ֜ה הַבָּקָ֣ר וְהַצֹּ֗אן אַֽל־יִטְעֲמוּ֙ מְא֔וּמָה
> אַל־יִרְע֕וּ וּמַ֖יִם אַל־יִשְׁתּֽוּ׃

וַיַּזְעֵ֗ק. Narrative discourse—mainline. Hiph *wayyiqtol* 3 m s.

וַיֹּ֙אמֶר֙ בְּנִֽינְוֵ֔ה מִטַּ֧עַם הַמֶּ֛לֶךְ וּגְדֹלָ֖יו לֵאמֹ֑ר. Narrative discourse—mainline.

וַיֹּ֙אמֶר֙. Qal *wayyiqtol* 3 m s. On the use of אָמַר as a discourse switch cue, see 1:6. The precise starting point of the king's edict has received much attention. The nature of the difficulty lies in the use of two quotative frames (אָמַר and לֵאמֹר) within the verse (and in close proximity). Most modern translations (NIV, NRSV, NJPS, NEB) begin the quotation after בְּנִֽינְוֵה. The ancient traditions had a much more difficult time in assigning the precise start of the quotation (see Sasson, 252–53). Throughout the book of Jonah the narrator has employed multiple verb-frames when introducing a quote (cf. 1:14), thus perhaps explaining the tendency of most translators in rendering this verse. Two points merit consideration, however, in determining the beginning of the quotation. A *zaqeph qaton* appears above בְּנִֽינְוֵה linking it with the first quotative frame. The *atnah* beneath לֵאמֹר may further support the notion that the first half of the verse is set off apart from the quotation itself which follows. Secondly, and more importantly, Miller (196) has demonstrated that in representations of speech where there are two matrix metapragmatic verbs (i.e., אָמַר and זָעַק) along with a לֵאמֹר frame, then the quote proper follows the

לֵאמֹר frame (other examples include Gen 39:14-15; Exod 15:1; Num 30:3-5; Josh 9:22-23; Judg 16:18b; 21:10-11).

בְּנִינְוֵה. The preposition בְּ indicates spatial localization—the so-called *beth locale*. The prepositional phrase is an adjunct to the verb.

מִטַּעַם. The noun טַעַם is usually translated as "taste" (cf. Exod 16:31) or more figuratively as "judgment" (cf. 1 Sam 25:33; Prov 11:22; 26:16; Job 12:20). Most translations of Jonah, however, opt for "decree," despite the fact that such usage fails to appear elsewhere in the Hebrew Bible (BDB, 381). The noun טַעַם is clearly meant as a pun on the first directive ("let them not taste"), hence explaining in part the appearance of the term. But equally important is the more figurative meaning of "judgment," also understood as "discernment" or "discretion." The narrator has consistently set up the faith of the foreign people (sailors, Ninevites, and king of Nineveh) as a foil to the lack of faith of Jonah. By translating the term טַעַם as "judgment," in the sense of proper discernment, the theme is reinforced.

The preposition מִן may be used "to mark the author or the authority from which a standard or truth originated" (WO, 213). Sasson attempts such a rendering with "on the authority of the kings and his counselors" (240). Unfortunately he includes the phrase within the larger quotation of the edict.

הַמֶּלֶךְ. Absolute noun of construct phrase.

וּגְדֹלָיו. Absolute noun of construct phrase. Normally two absolute nouns cannot be governed by a single construct noun. In such cases, the construct noun is usually repeated (cf. Gen 24:3). The construct noun, however, need not be repeated if the two absolute nouns are closely related, as in the present case (MNK, 195).

Trible suggests that the use of וּגְדֹלָיו here and מִגְּדוֹלָם earlier in 3:5 may be an effort to connect both the popular and the royal responses.

לֵאמֹר. Prep + Qal inf constr. The infinitive operates as a complementizer standing at the end of the quotative frame. The complementizer also serves as a discourse switch cue.

הָאָדָם וְהַבְּהֵמָה הַבָּקָר וְהַצֹּאן אַל־יִטְעֲמוּ מְאוּמָה. Embedded hortatory discourse—off-the-line. Although not a volitive, and
hence off the mainline, the אַל + *yiqtol* remains high on the profile
scheme for hortatory discourse (see Introduction). The construction
is meant to express prohibitive commands, thus continuing the goal
of hortatory discourse to alter or change the behavior of another. Van
der Merwe, Naudé, and Kroeze refer to this type of construction as
a "direct directive," explaining that "direct directives indicate explic-
itly that they wish their listeners to adjust their behavior accordingly"
(149). See 1:14 on mitigated hortatory speech.

הָאָדָם וְהַבְּהֵמָה. Together, the two terms form a merismus, yet
each serves separately as the subject for each of the first two verbs.

הַבָּקָר וְהַצֹּאן. A second merismus appears, qualifying the second
term in the previous merismus, הַבְּהֵמָה. As opposed to all living animals, the royal declaration applies only to herds of cattle or flocks of
sheep and goats.

אַל־יִטְעֲמוּ. Neg part + Qal *yiqtol* 3 m p (jussive). Elsewhere in the
Hebrew Bible, the verb טָעַם appears with humans as the subject of
the verb. Hence, the first prohibition relates to the first element in the
first merismus.

מְאוּמָה. Indefinite pronoun serving as direct object.

אַל־יִרְעוּ. Embedded hortatory discourse—off-the-line. Neg part +
Qal *yiqtol* 3 m p from רָעָה (jussive). On the function of a אַל + *yiqtol*
in hortatory discourse and direct directives, see above. Similar to the
particular use of טָעַם with human subjects, the verb רָעָה appears
with only animals as its subject, thus indicating that the second prohibition appears directed at the second element in the merismus.

וּמַיִם אַל־יִשְׁתּוּ. Embedded hortatory discourse—off-the-line. On
the function of אַל + *yiqtol* in hortatory discourse and the notion of
direct directives, see above.

מַיִם. Direct object of יִשְׁתּוּ.

אַל־יִשְׁתּוּ. Neg particle + Qal *yiqtol* 3 m p from שָׁתָה (jussive). The final prohibition breaks with the two earlier prohibitions in the verse, noted in part by the fronting of the direct object. The totality expressed in the first merismus may in fact be the subject of the final prohibition. In other words, הָאָדָם וְהַבְּהֵמָה as a unit may be in view in the final prohibition.

3:8 וְיִתְכַּסּוּ שַׂקִּים הָאָדָם וְהַבְּהֵמָה וְיִקְרְאוּ אֶל־אֱלֹהִים בְּחָזְקָה וְיָשֻׁבוּ אִישׁ מִדַּרְכּוֹ הָרָעָה וּמִן־הֶחָמָס אֲשֶׁר בְּכַפֵּיהֶם׃

וְיִתְכַּסּוּ שַׂקִּים הָאָדָם וְהַבְּהֵמָה. Embedded hortatory discourse—mainline. A clause-initial jussive form of the verb כָּסָה returns the discourse to the mainline. The shift from off-the-line to mainline is difficult to express in translation given the high ranking of the אַל + *yiqtol* form in the hortatory profile scheme.

וְיִתְכַּסּוּ. *Waw* cop + Hithpael *yiqtol* 3 m p כָּסָה (jussive). The *waw* copulative is frequently employed in connecting volitional forms. Wolff has suggested that verse 8 is meant to extend the satirical tone of the book (152–53). According to Wolff, the Hithpael form of כָּסָה is reflexive, thus leading to the absurd image of both humans and animals covering themselves in sackcloth (הָאָדָם וְהַבְּהֵמָה). While possible, an alternative suggestion seems more plausible. The narrator may have intentionally repeated the merismus for literary balance in verse 8. In verse 7, the merismus appears along with three prohibitions, and equally so, in verse 8, the merismus appears along with three injunctions.

שַׂקִּים. Direct object of וְיִתְכַּסּוּ.

הָאָדָם וְהַבְּהֵמָה. Subject of וְיִתְכַּסּוּ.

וְיִקְרְאוּ אֶל־אֱלֹהִים בְּחָזְקָה. Embedded hortatory discourse—
mainline. The volitive sense is continued by the use of the *waw* copulative with a jussive.

וְיִקְרְאוּ. *Waw* cop + Qal *yiqtol* 3 m p (jussive). In Jonah, the construction קְרָא אֶל followed by a divine name indicates an act of invo-
cation to the deity. The phrase appears in conjunction with the sailors
(1:5, 14), the captain (1:6), the Ninevites (3:8), and even Jonah himself (2:3, although the divine name shifts to יְהוָה).

אֶל־אֱלֹהִים. The prepositional phrase functions as a complement
to the verb, marking out the goal of the saying process.

בְּחָזְקָה. The prepositional phrase is an adjunct to the verb, functioning as an adverbial modifier. In the other four uses of קְרָא אֶל,
there is not a prepositional phrase functioning adverbially. Sasson suggests that its insertion here is not simply fortuitous, but may in fact,
serve as a device "to gauge the depth of a worshiper's conviction,"
further preparing the reader for the radical call for repentance in the
subsequent clause (258).

וְיָשֻׁבוּ אִישׁ מִדַּרְכּוֹ הָרָעָה וּמִן־הֶחָמָס. Embedded hortatory
discourse—mainline.

וְיָשֻׁבוּ. *Waw* cop + Qal *yiqtol* 3 m p from שׁוּב. The use of שׁוּב in
verse 8 further heightens the ambiguity surrounding the initial proclamation of Jonah that Nineveh would be "overturned" (הָפַךְ).

אִישׁ. On the use of the collective noun as subject of a plural verb,
see 1:5.

מִדַּרְכּוֹ הָרָעָה. The preposition indicates spatial positioning,
denoting movement away from an object. The noun דֶּרֶךְ operates
as both masculine and feminine in Hebrew. As a result, the word
הָרָעָה may be understood as either a feminine adjective modifying a
feminine noun (Snaith, 34), or as a feminine noun apparently standing in apposition to דֶּרֶךְ (Owens, 837). Given that apposition appears
more regularly in BH than in English, one may argue that the latter

position is the preferable one, understanding that the two elements
are functioning as a clausal constituent (object of the preposition).
The second member of the phrase reveals a quality or characteristic
concerning the first element, but may be better translated adjectively
(MNK, 228). On the nature of noun-noun appositional phrases, see
WO, 229–32.

וּמִן־הֶחָמָס. When a preposition governs more than one object,
the preposition will typically be repeated before each object. The *waw*
copulative + מִן signals the continuation of the prepositional phrase.

אֲשֶׁר בְּכַפֵּיהֶם. Embedded hortatory discourse—off-the-line. The
relative pronoun אֲשֶׁר introduces a subordinate clause meant to provide additional information.

אֲשֶׁר. The antecedent to the relative pronoun is הֶחָמָס, and it
serves as the subject of the subordinate clause.

בְּכַפֵּיהֶם. The preposition indicates spatial localization, and is frequently labeled a *beth locale*. Virtually all of the translations attempt
to remedy the apparent discrepancy in the pronominal suffixes found
in the two prepositional phrases: מִדַּרְכּוֹ and בְּכַפֵּיהֶם. For example,
the NRSV, NAB, JPS, NASB, and the JB all convert the 3 m p suffix
into a singular so that it will mirror the 3 m s suffix in the previous
phrase. Rather than glossing over the discrepancy in pronominal suffixes, Trible suggests that the two phrases are meant to be understood
as an example of synthetic parallelism, and thus the switching in pronominal suffixes is meant for effect. She writes, "The pronominal suffixes 'his' and 'their' fix responsibility individually and corporately,
and the nouns 'way' and 'hands' signify the means" (1994, 186).

3:9   מִי־יוֹדֵעַ יָשׁוּב וְנִחַם הָאֱלֹהִים וְשָׁב מֵחֲרוֹן אַפּוֹ וְלֹא
נֹאבֵד: מִי־יוֹדֵעַ

מִי־יוֹדֵעַ יָשׁוּב וְנִחַם הָאֱלֹהִים. Embedded hortatory discourse—off-the-line. If מִי־יוֹדֵעַ is understood as a fixed expression (see below), then the clause is an X + *yiqtol* form. In hortatory discouse, *yiqtol* verb forms tend to express possibility.

מִי־יוֹדֵעַ. Interrog pronoun – Qal act ptc m s. The interrogative followed by a participle is best understood as an exclamatory expression, particularly when it appears at the head of a sentence. Van der Merwe, Naudé, and Kroeze suggest that the two words actually operate in tandem as a "fixed expression," with the primary intent being that of expressing a wish for which the outcome appears questionable (323). In his study of the phrase, Crenshaw observed that the phrase stands of the head of the sentence in four instances (2 Sam 12:22; Joel 2:14; Ps 90:11; Jonah 3:9), and elsewhere in the Hebrew Bible 6 times. Particularly when the phrase stands at the beginning of the phrase, it may be understood as synonymous with the prophetic אוּלַי, hence matching the claim of the king in 3:9 with that of the captain in 1:6 (Crenshaw, 276).

יָשׁוּב. Qal *yiqtol* 3 m s. A *zaqeph qaton* appears above יָשׁוּב, suggesting that the verb be read with the opening phrase. Were such a division adopted, the phrase would read "He who knows will turn back." Yet in Joel 2:14, the verse begins with the same four words as in Jonah 3:9, but marked differently. Based on the location of the disjunctive marker in Joel 2, the phrase מִי־יוֹדֵעַ is understood as a fixed expression separate from יָשׁוּב, with the entire clause being understood as a desiderative clause. Routinely in the Hebrew Bible, a desiderative clause begins with an exclamation (most notably מִי) coupled with a verb in the volitive mood (GKC, 476–77; AC, 190). By disregarding the disjunctive marker in 3:9, the clause more closely resembles that speech of the captain in 1:6—אוּלַי followed by a *yiqtol* understood in the volitive mood.

וְנִחַם. *Waw* cop + Niph *qatal* 3 m s. When a jussive is followed by a *weqatal*, the intent is often to express a consequent situation, whether

logical or chronological (WO, 529). Thus the actions implied by the
two verbs שׁוּב and נָחַם should not construed as occurring simulta-
neously (i.e., the coordinate force of the *waw*), but instead should be
understood as sequential.

הָאֱלֹהִים. Subject of both יָשׁוּב and נִחַם.

וְשָׁב מֵחֲרוֹן אַפּוֹ. Embedded hortatory discourse—off-the-line. As
with וְנִחַם, the *weqatal* is meant to express a consequent situation,
whether logical or chronological (WO, 529).

וְשָׁב. *Waw* cop + Qal *qatal* 3 m s from שׁוּב. The earlier *yiqtol*,
יָשׁוּב, establishes the condition, while the latter two verbs (וְנִחַם and
וְשָׁב) indicate the desired wish or outcome predicated upon that initial condition. Sasson notes that in similar phrases employing מִי־
יוֹדֵעַ, a condition is expressed with a *yiqtol*, followed by the expressed
wish (typically as a cohortative or *weqatal* [260–61]). Jonah 3:9 is the
only time this construction is expanded, indicating not one, but two
desired outcomes.

מֵחֲרוֹן אַפּוֹ. The preposition indicates spatial positioning, denoting movement away from an object. The construct phrase expresses a
relationship of possession. Possessive pronoun.

וְלֹא נֹאבֵד. Embedded hortatory discourse—off-the-line. *Waw* cop +
neg – Qal *yiqtol* 1 c p. A לֹא + *yiqtol* construction moves the discourse
off the mainline, offering a consequence or purpose statement. The
waw in this instance refers to the result of the content of the preceding
clause (MNK, 299). As a result, rather than translating the waw as the
simple conjunction "and," the waw might be better translated as "in
order that" or "so that."

Jonah 3:10

[10] And then God saw their deeds, how they had turned from their
evil way, and he changed his mind concerning the disaster which he
had promised to do to them and he did not do it.

3:10 וַיַּ֤רְא הָֽאֱלֹהִים֙ אֶֽת־מַ֣עֲשֵׂיהֶ֔ם כִּי־שָׁ֖בוּ מִדַּרְכָּ֣ם הָרָעָ֑ה
וַיִּנָּ֣חֶם הָאֱלֹהִ֗ים עַל־הָרָעָ֛ה אֲשֶׁר־דִּבֶּ֥ר לַעֲשׂוֹת־לָהֶ֖ם
וְלֹ֥א עָשָֽׂה׃

וַיַּ֤רְא הָֽאֱלֹהִים֙ אֶֽת־מַ֣עֲשֵׂיהֶ֔ם. Narrative discourse—mainline.
The *wayyiqtol* serves as a discourse switch clue.

וַיַּ֤רְא. Qal *wayyiqtol* 3 m s from רָאָה.

הָֽאֱלֹהִים֙. Subject of וַיַּ֤רְא.

אֶֽת־מַ֣עֲשֵׂיהֶ֔ם. Direct object of וַיַּ֤רְא. The root עָשָׂה appears three
times in verse 10, subtly noting the connection between the "deeds"
of the Ninevites, Yahweh's promise "to do" them in, and his refusal to
carry out his judgment.

כִּי־שָׁ֖בוּ מִדַּרְכָּ֣ם הָרָעָ֑ה. Narrative discourse—off-the-line. The
particle introduces an object clause.

כִּי. Subordinating conjunction.

שָׁ֖בוּ. Qal *qatal* 3 c p from שׁוּב.

מִדַּרְכָּ֣ם הָרָעָ֑ה. On the identification of הָרָעָה as a noun or adjective, as well as issues related to noun-noun apposition, see 3:8.

וַיִּנָּ֣חֶם הָאֱלֹהִ֗ים עַל־הָרָעָ֛ה. Narrative discourse—mainline.

וַיִּנָּ֣חֶם. Niphal *wayyiqtol* 3 m s. A nearly identical phrase appears
in Exodus 32:14, when God decides to withhold judgment from his
people.

הָאֱלֹהִ֗ים. Subject of וַיִּנָּ֣חֶם.

עַל־הָרָעָ֛ה. The preposition indicates specification related to a
particular topic ("concerning").

אֲשֶׁר־דִּבֶּ֥ר לַעֲשׂוֹת־לָהֶ֖ם. Narrative discourse—off-the-line. A *qatal*
in a dependent clause provides background information in the relative

past (i.e., past in comparison to the mainline). This is often expressed in translation through the use of a pluperfect (Longacre, 82).

אֲשֶׁר. Rel pronoun. The antecedent (הָרָעָה) is the object of the relative clause.

דִּבֶּר. Piel *qatal* 3 m s.

לַעֲשׂוֹת. Prep + Qal inf constr. The infinitive functions as a complement to the main verb in the clause. Although דִּבֶּר is frequently followed by a preposition (primarily עִם, לְ, אֶל, and אֵת), an infinitive may follow the verb in order to complete the idea expressed in the main verb (cf. Exod 32:14; Deut 1:4; 19:8; 2 Kgs 14:27; Ezek 6:10).

לָהֶם. The prepositional phrase functions as a complement to לַעֲשׂוֹת, with the preposition marking the indirect object. Objective pronoun.

וְלֹא עָשָׂה. Narrative discourse—off-the-line. *Waw* cop + neg – Qal *qatal* 3 m s. Typically in narrative discourse, the negation of any verb is understood as *irrealis* scene setting and appears at the lowest level on the discourse profile scheme. The negation of a verb stops the forward progress of the narrative by indicating what is not the case. Longacre, however, has suggested that in certain contexts a negation may be termed a "momentous negation" because it is critical in advancing the narrative line forward (82). In these rare occurrences, the verb form is understood as a second-rank construction (similar to the X + *qatal*), in effect actually serving to move the narrative along. The events and dialog in chapter 4 are predicated, in part, on the momentous negation that occurs at the end of 3:10. The object of the verb is absent due to ellipsis.

Jonah 4:1-4

¹Now Jonah was greatly displeased and angered. ²And then he prayed to the LORD, "O please, LORD, was this not my word when I was still in my land? Therefore, I hastened to flee to Tarshish because

I knew that you are a gracious and compassionate God, slow to anger and abundant in steadfast love, and one who relents concerning disaster. ³Therefore, O LORD, please take my life from me for my death is preferable to my life." ⁴And then the LORD said, "Is your being angry right?"

4:1   וַיֵּרַע אֶל־יוֹנָה רָעָה גְדוֹלָה וַיִּחַר לוֹ:

וַיֵּרַע אֶל־יוֹנָה רָעָה גְדוֹלָה. Narrative discourse—mainline.

וַיֵּרַע. Qal *wayyiqtol* 3 m s from רָעַע. The verb וַיֵּרַע is an impersonal construction. In expressing emotions or experiences, frequently an impersonal construction appears (primarily in the Qal stem). In such constructions, there is no topic or subject in view beyond that expressed in the predicate (WO, 377). The narrator continues the use of רָעָה but in verbal form. The verb serves to transition the narrative from chapter three to chapter four. The use of רָעָה in 3:8 and 3:10 to describe the Ninevite's ways is countered by Yahweh's turning or repenting of רָעָה in 3:10. This, however, leads to Jonah's state of רָעַע in 4:1 (Magonet, 24).

אֶל־יוֹנָה. In an impersonal construction, the verb + אֶל (or לְ as below) indicates the one who is experiencing the emotion. The construction might also signal that the source of the emotion is coming from outside the individual (as opposed to anger "welling up within"), although Waltke and O'Connor caution against an exaggeration of this point (377).

רָעָה גְדוֹלָה. רָעָה is an internal adjunct (often referred to as a *schema etymologicum, figura etymologica*, or internal object). The function of such a construction is to describe the intensity of the verbal idea.

וַיִּחַר לוֹ. Narrative discourse—mainline.

וַיִּחַר. Qal *wayyiqtol* 3 m s from חָרָה. As in the first clause, this clause contains the same referent for the impersonal subject, and hence should probably be rendered similarly (contra Wolff, 159). The verb operates in Janus-like fashion. חָרָה extends the notion of Jonah's displeasure (also expressed in 4:4) as expressed earlier in the verb רָעַע, but also points forward to verse 9 in which Jonah is "heated up" as a result of the sun.

לֹו. On the function of the preposition in impersonal constructions, see above (אֶל־יֹונָה). Objective pronoun.

4:2   וַיִּתְפַּלֵּל אֶל־יְהוָֹה וַיֹּאמַר אָנָּה יְהוָֹה הֲלוֹא־זֶה
דְבָרִי עַד־הֱיוֹתִי עַל־אַדְמָתִי עַל־כֵּן קִדַּמְתִּי לִבְרֹחַ
תַּרְשִׁישָׁה כִּי יָדַעְתִּי כִּי אַתָּה אֵל־חַנּוּן וְרַחוּם אֶרֶךְ
אַפַּיִם וְרַב־חֶסֶד וְנִחָם עַל־הָרָעָה:

וַיִּתְפַּלֵּל אֶל־יְהוָה. Narrative discourse—mainline.

וַיִּתְפַּלֵּל. Hithpael *wayyiqtol* 3 m s. Sequential use of the *wayyiqtol*.

אֶל־יְהוָה. The prepositional phrase functions as a complement to the verb, marking out the goal of the saying process.

וַיֹּאמַר. Narrative discourse—mainline. Qal *wayyiqtol* 3 m s. In this case, the clause serves two purposes. First, as a *wayyiqtol* form, the verb extends the mainline of the narrative. Second, the chosen verb (אָמַר) actually serves as a discourse switch cue, signaling the transition from one discourse (narrative discourse) to another (embedded hortatory discourse).

Again, the narrator in Jonah opts for multiple verbs in the quotative frame. Miller notes that the "central configuration" (most commonly occurring verbal construction) of פָּלַל is that of a multiple verb frame (307). As is frequently the case with multiple verbs in the quotative frame, the first verb relates the manner in which the speech is given, and the second, marks the beginning of the actual speech itself (Rocine, 10).

אָנָּה יְהוָה הֲלוֹא־זֶה דְבָרִי. Embedded hortatory discourse—off-the-line. Verbless clauses typically provide background or explanatory information in hortatory discourse.

אָנָּה יְהוָה. Vocative. The same phrase occurs in 1:14. As in 1:14, the vocative functions as an adjunct, syntactically separate from the remainder of the clause.

הֲלוֹא־זֶה דְבָרִי. The interrogative part + neg part introduces a rhetorical question that results in a statement that cannot be easily challenged by the addressee (MNK, 322). Thus the question is not meant to illicit information, rather it provides a type of indictment.

עַד־הֱיוֹתִי עַל־אַדְמָתִי. Embedded hortatory discourse—off-the-line. The clause functions as a temporal adjunct, meant to explain or qualify the previous clause.

עַד־הֱיוֹתִי. Prep – Qal inf constr + 1 c s suffix. The pronominal suffix serves as the subject of the infinitive clause. In a temporal infinitive clause, the clause may best be translated in a subordinate clause construction.

עַל־אַדְמָתִי. Spatial use of the preposition.

עַל־כֵּן קִדַּמְתִּי. Embedded hortatory discourse—off-the-line. The appearance of a *qatal* within a dependent clause suggests that the activity presented in the clause occurred in the past (relative to the time of the mainline).

עַל־כֵּן. Among its many functions, the construction עַל־כֵּן may serve to establish a causal link between two clauses.

קִדַּמְתִּי. Piel *qatal* 1 c s. As Sasson has noted, the narrator's use of קָדַם results in an unusual construction. He explains, "there is good reason to believe that the narrator coined it precisely for this context. The verbal form *librōah* instantly takes us back to that precise moment that Jonah moved in a direction opposite to his intended itinerary" as articulated in 1:3 (278). קָדַם typically refers to coming prior to something else (BDB, 869), but in the present context, it appears to function as a *verbum relativum* with the infinitive (cf. Wolff, 160). When קָדַם is followed by a לְ + infinitive, the phrase may be understood as anticipatory (Holladay, 312), perhaps rendering the Hebrew, "Therefore I hastened to flee." The LXX attempts to capture this rendering with δια τουτο προεφθασα του φυγειν ("because of this, I anticipated fleeing").

לִבְרֹחַ תַּרְשִׁישָׁה. Embedded hortatory discourse—off-the-line.

לִבְרֹחַ. Prep + Qal inf constr. See 1:3. The infinitive creates a subordinate purpose clause to קִדַּמְתִּי.

תַּרְשִׁישָׁה. The word functions adverbially in the clause.

כִּי יָדַעְתִּי. Embedded hortatory discourse—off-the-line. In hortatory discourse, a verbal clause containing a *qatal* not only moves the narrative off the mainline, it introduces information that is either explanatory or background.

כִּי יָדַעְתִּי. Conj – Qal *qatal* 1 c s. כִּי introduces a causal clause.

כִּי אַתָּה אֵל־חַנּוּן וְרַחוּם אֶרֶךְ אַפַּיִם וְרַב־חֶסֶד וְנִחָם עַל־הָרָעָה. Embedded expository discourse—mainline. Hebrew typically embeds one discourse type in another through the use of a subordinating particle (כִּי). In this case, the narrator has embedded expository discourse within hortatory discourse. As Garrett has noted, an embedded discourse can appear prominent in the text (321). Here the verbless clause provides not only a description of the deity, but more particularly, a culminating rationale to the fleeing of Jonah mentioned earlier in the verse.

כִּי אַתָּה. When כִּי follows the verb יָדַע, it introduces an object clause and may be translated as the subordinating conjunction "that."

The object clause is comprised of four "lexemes presented in parallel. . . . Each lexeme evokes equivalent but different aspects of meaning within a greater domain of affective qualities" (Kamp, 181). Hence, the noun clause is not intended as a list of individual divine qualities, but rather, taken together, they intend to generate a characterization of God. For an identical listing see Joel 2:13.

אֵל־חַנּוּן. Note the "firm or indispensable *meteg*" beneath אֵל. The accent mark retains a long vowel that appears before a closed syllable prior to a *maqqeph* (GKC, 64). Without the accent mark, the vowel would be reduced to a *sᵉghol*.

וְרַחוּם. The *zaqeph qaton* that appears above וְרַחוּם signals that the term is meant to be read in conjunction with אֵל־חַנּוּן. Hence the waw does not introduce a new phrase, but rather, connects רַחוּם to אֵל.

אֶרֶךְ אַפַּיִם. Epexegetical construct phrase. The construct noun characterizes the absolute noun.

וְרַב־חֶסֶד. Epexegetical construct phrase.

וְנִחָם. *Waw* cop + Niphal ptc. Substantive use of the participle.

עַל־הָרָעָה. The indicates specification of topic. Note again the narrator's use of the root רָעָה.

4:3 וְעַתָּה יְהֹוָה קַח־נָא אֶת־נַפְשִׁי מִמֶּנִּי כִּי טוֹב מוֹתִי מֵחַיָּי׃

וְעַתָּה יְהֹוָה קַח־נָא אֶת־נַפְשִׁי מִמֶּנִּי. Embedded hortatory discourse—off-the-line. Although the main verb in the clause is an imperative, which typically signifies a mainline clause, the structure of the clause is X + imperative, thus moving the clause off-the-line.

וְעַתָּה. The temporal adverb עַתָּה, when joined with a *waw*, functions as a discourse marker, frequently indicating a logical conclusion (WO, 667; MNK, 333). The plea in verse 3 is predicated upon the claims of Jonah in verse 2.

יְהֹוָה. On the function of the vocative, see 1:14. Here, however, the noun is not an adjunct, but instead is the subject of the imperative.

קַח־נָא. Qal impv 2 m s from לָקַח – particle of entreaty.

אֶת־נַפְשִׁי. Direct object. Possessive pronoun.

מִמֶּנִּי. The preposition indicates spatial positioning, denoting movement away from an object.

כִּי טוֹב מוֹתִי מֵחַיָּי. Embedded hortatory discourse—off-the-line. In hortatory discourse, verbless clauses are merely scene setting clauses, meant to offer background information for the preceding clause. The comments in this clause are intended as an explanatory statement for the request in the previous clause.

כִּי. Conj.

טוֹב מוֹתִי מֵחַיָּי. The causal clause is comprised of a positive comparison employing the comparative מִן (טוֹב + x + מִן + y = "x is better than y"). Possessive use of the pronouns. The LXX, Old Latin, and the Syriac convert the nouns into infinitives, "it is better for me to live than to die." The NRSV, NIV, and the JPS follow similarly, and opt to construct the comparison using verbs. The translation above attempts to render the usage of nouns in the Hebrew.

4:4   וַיֹּאמֶר יְהֹוָה הַהֵיטֵב חָרָה לָךְ:

וַיֹּאמֶר יְהֹוָה. Narrative discourse—mainline. The *wayyiqtol* form of the verb indicates a return from direct speech (embedded hortatory discourse) to narrative discourse. Once again, however, the verb operates as a discourse switch clue, returning to direct speech discourse.

וַיֹּאמֶר. Qal *wayyiqtol* 3 m s.

יְהֹוָה. Subject of וַיֹּאמֶר.

הַהֵיטֵב חָרָה לָךְ. Embedded expository discourse—off-the-line. The direct speech can be classified as expository. The thesis, or central point of the statement, is placed in a rhetorical question (see 4:2). In the X + *qatal* construction, הֵיטֵב is fronted, and in so doing, focuses the question on whether such anger is justified.

הַהֵיטֵב. Interrogative *he* + Hiph inf abs. The infinitive absolute appears as an adverbial modifier of the main verb in the clause. Such a use of the infinitive is dictated by the lexical value of the stem in the infinitive. As in the present case, most adverbial usages of the infinitive absolute occur in the Hiphil (MNK, 160; Wolff, 160, 169). Whereas the rhetorical question in 4:2, using הֲלוֹא, anticipates a positive assent, the rhetorical question employing הֲ anticipates a negative assent.

חָרָה. Qal *qatal* 3 m s. As in 4:1, חָרָה appears in an impersonal construction. In 4:1, however, the verb appears as a *wayyiqtol*, whereas the present clause contains an X + *qatal* form. As Niccacci has observed, frequently an event is first narrated using the *wayyiqtol* form and then reported in direct speech using a *qatal* form (180).

לְךָ. See 4:1.

Jonah 4:5-7

⁵And then Jonah went out of the city and sat just east of it. There he built for himself a booth and he sat under it in the shade until he could see what would happen in the city. ⁶Then the LORD God appointed a plant and it grew up over Jonah to be shade for his head in order to deliver him from his calamity. And Jonah was exceedingly glad concerning the plant. ⁷As dawn was breaking on the next day, God appointed a worm and it attacked the plant and it withered.

4:5 וַיֵּצֵא יוֹנָה מִן־הָעִיר וַיֵּשֶׁב מִקֶּדֶם לָעִיר וַיַּעַשׂ לוֹ שָׁם
סֻכָּה וַיֵּשֶׁב תַּחְתֶּיהָ בַּצֵּל עַד אֲשֶׁר יִרְאֶה מַה־יִּהְיֶה
בָּעִיר׃

וַיֵּצֵא יוֹנָה מִן־הָעִיר. Narrative discourse—mainline.

וַיֵּצֵא. Qal *wayyiqtol* 3 m s. The *wayyiqtol* form returns the narrative to the mainline. The events outlined in verse 5, however, have raised considerable discussion as to how one should translate the opening *wayyiqtol*. Following Lohfink's (1961) suggestion that the book of Jonah contains several "flashbacks," Wolff has opted to render the *wayyiqtol* as a pluperfect ("For Jonah had gone out of the city"; cf. Wolff, 169). Given that *wayyiqtols* function as pluperfects only rarely (1 Kgs 13:12), the notion of the clause as a flashback should probably be abandoned. Instead, the *wayyiqtol* should be understood as introducing a new section of narrative in the storyline. Such a use of the *wayyiqtol* is accompanied by an introduction of the new characters as well as a change of location. In addition, verbs of motion (יצא) frequently appear with this type of use (MNK, 166). In the NRSV, the translators grouped verse 5 with the preceding four verses (hence ignoring the possibility of a new section of narrative), yet they do abandon the notion of the verb as a pluperfect. In the JPS, a new narrative begins in verse 5, yet the verb is still translated as a pluperfect. The clause should be understood as introducing a new narrative within the story, absent of any sense of "flashback."

יוֹנָה. Subject of וַיֵּצֵא.

מִן־הָעִיר. The preposition indicates spatial positioning, denoting movement away from an object.

וַיֵּשֶׁב מִקֶּדֶם לָעִיר. Narrative discourse—mainline.

וַיֵּשֶׁב. Qal *wayyiqtol* 3 m s.

מִקֶּדֶם. Similar to the verb חָרָה in 4:1, the noun קֶדֶם appears to operate in Janus-like fashion, connecting Jonah's decision "to hasten to flee" (קִדַּמְתִּי) with the "east" (קָדִים) wind in verse 8. It is worth noting that קֶדֶם was the direction the disobedient moved throughout the Primeval history (Gen 3:24; 4:16; 11:2).

לָעִיר. Spatial sense of the preposition.

וַיַּעַשׂ לוֹ שָׁם סֻכָּה. Narrative discourse—mainline.

וַיַּעַשׂ. Qal *wayyiqtol* 3 m s from עָשָׂה.

לוֹ. Because the pronominal suffix agrees in number and gender with the subject of the verb, the construction is frequently referred to as an ethical dative, with some (GKC, 381) opting to speak of it as apparently pleonastic. More recent work has sought to emphasize the reflexive nature of the construction, which appears to be the primary function in the present verse. Objective use of pronoun.

שָׁם. Adverb. Although deictic adverbs will stand as close to the verb as possible, they will, nonetheless, follow the preposition + pronominal suffix construction.

סֻכָּה. Direct object of וַיַּעַשׂ.

וַיֵּשֶׁב תַּחְתֶּיהָ בַּצֵּל. Narrative discourse—mainline.

וַיֵּשֶׁב. Qal *wayyiqtol* 3 m s.

תַּחְתֶּיהָ. The prepositional phrase is an adjunct, functioning in a locative sense. The antecedent to the pronoun is סֻכָּה.

בַּצֵּל. The preposition בְּ indicates spatial localization—the so-called *beth locale*.

עַד אֲשֶׁר יִרְאֶה. Narrative discourse—off-the-line. The clause stands in a subordinate relationship with the previous clause. The presence of a *yiqtol*, however, within the clause indicates that the storyline has shifted from the mainline of the narrative to non-past background information. In addition, the *yiqtol* indicates modality, stressing the possibility or potentiality of events (MNK, 148–49).

עַד אֲשֶׁר. The preposition is used temporally, marking a point in time up to which something occurs ("until").

יִרְאֶה. Qal *yiqtol* 3 m s.

מַה־יִּהְיֶה בָּעִיר. Narrative discourse—off-the-line. The clause functions as an object clause to the main verb in the preceding clause

(יִרְאֶה). As with the previous clause, the *yiqtol* indicates that the narrative is off-the-line, thus continuing to provide the reader with nonpast background material. The notion of modality continues.

מַה־יִּהְיֶה. Indefinite pronoun + Qal *yiqtol* 3 m s. Although מַה frequently appears as an interrogative, it can also appear as an indefinite pronoun. Here the pronoun stands as the subject of יִהְיֶה.

בָּעִיר. The preposition בְּ indicates spatial localization—the so-called *beth locale*.

4:6 וַיְמַן יְהוָה־אֱלֹהִים קִיקָיוֹן | מֵעַל לְיוֹנָה לִהְיוֹת צֵל עַל־רֹאשׁוֹ לְהַצִּיל לוֹ מֵרָעָתוֹ וַיִּשְׂמַח יוֹנָה עַל־הַקִּיקָיוֹן שִׂמְחָה גְדוֹלָה :

וַיְמַן יְהוָה־אֱלֹהִים קִיקָיוֹן. Narrative discourse—mainline.

וַיְמַן. Piel *wayyiqtol* 3 m s from מָנָה. See 2:1.

יְהוָה־אֱלֹהִים. Although both divine names have appeared individually throughout the book of Jonah, it is only in 4:6 that they appear together. On the use of divine names in Jonah, see Kamp (124–25).

קִיקָיוֹן. Direct object of וַיְמַן.

וַיַּעַל מֵעַל לְיוֹנָה. Narrative discourse—mainline.

וַיַּעַל. Qal *wayyiqtol* 3 m s from עָלָה. Several translations (NRSV; TEV; TNIV) consider יְהוָה־אֱלֹהִים to be the subject, thus apparently reading וַיַּעַל as a Hiphil *wayyiqtol*. Morphologically, the form could be parsed as a Hiphil, yet when עָלָה appears in conjunction with vegetation, the preferred form is the Qal (BDB, 748; Snaith, 38), thus precluding a causative sense (cf. NASB).

מֵעַל לְיוֹנָה. The phrase מֵעַל לְ is best understood as "over," "up over," or "above," hence producing a prepositional phrase which stands as an adjunct, functioning locatively.

לִהְיוֹת צֵל עַל־רֹאשׁוּ. Narrative discourse—mainline. The infinitive construct coupled with a לְ introduces a subordinate purpose clause. The phrase is meant to explain the statements made in the main clause.

לִהְיוֹת. Prep + Qal inf constr from הָיָה.

צֵל. Object of the purpose clause.

עַל־רֹאשׁוּ. The preposition is understood locatively, with the prepositional phrase functioning as an adjunct to the verb. Possessive pronoun.

לְהַצִּיל לוֹ מֵרָעָתוֹ. Narrative discourse—mainline. The infinitive construct introduces a subordinate purpose clause. The appearance of two infinitive clauses in an asyndectic construction is somewhat unusual, but may be explained due to assonance. In the first infinitive clause, a לְ (from לִהְיוֹת) is followed by צֵל. In the second infinitive clause, the same sounds are repeated with the infinitive construct, לְהַצִּיל (Trible, 1994, 210).

לְהַצִּיל. Prep + Hiph inf constr from נָצַל.

לוֹ. The prepositional phrase functions as a complement to the verb, with the preposition marking the object of the verb. Objective pronoun.

מֵרָעָתוֹ. The preposition may be understood as a privative (MNK, 288), indicating alienation or separation from a perceived threat. Objective use of pronoun. The narrator returns to the semantically rich term רָעָה. The same term was employed in 1:2, 3:8, and 3:10 to refer to the actions of the Ninevites. In a different sense, it appeared in 3:10 referencing what Yahweh had promised to do to the city of Nineveh. In 4:1, both the noun and verbal forms of the word are employed to speak of Jonah's emotional state following Yahweh's turning from the רָעָה he had promised. Here, the author returns to the same term, but clearly referring to the calamity produced from his current circumstance.

וַיִּשְׂמַ֨ח יוֹנָ֤ה עַל־הַקִּֽיקָיוֹן֙ שִׂמְחָ֣ה גְדוֹלָ֔ה. Narrative discourse—mainline.

וַיִּשְׂמַ֨ח. Qal *wayyiqtol* 3 m s.

יוֹנָ֤ה. Subject of וַיִּשְׂמַ֨ח.

עַל־הַקִּֽיקָיוֹן֙. The preposition indicates specification of topic.

שִׂמְחָ֣ה גְדוֹלָ֔ה. שִׂמְחָ֣ה is an internal adjunct. See 1:10.

4:7　וַיְמַ֣ן הָאֱלֹהִים֩ תּוֹלַ֜עַת בַּעֲל֥וֹת הַשַּׁ֛חַר לַֽמָּחֳרָ֖ת וַתַּ֥ךְ אֶת־הַקִּֽיקָי֖וֹן וַיִּיבָֽשׁ׃

וַיְמַ֣ן הָאֱלֹהִים֩ תּוֹלַ֜עַת. Narrative discourse—mainline.

וַיְמַ֣ן. See 4:6

הָאֱלֹהִים֩. Subject of וַיְמַ֣ן.

תּוֹלַ֜עַת. Direct object of וַיְמַ֣ן.

בַּעֲל֥וֹת הַשַּׁ֛חַר לַֽמָּחֳרָ֖ת. Narrative discourse—mainline. The infinitive construct coupled with the preposition בְּ introduces a temporal clause that is subordinate to the main clause.

בַּעֲל֥וֹת. Prep + Qal inf constr from עָלָה. The use of a בְּ with the infinitive implies that the action in the temporal clause may be simultaneous with that action of the main clause. To be more precise, the phrase is simultaneous "in the sense that the action referred to by the בְּ + infinitive construction constitutes a stretch of time within which the action in the main clause takes place" (MNK, 148–49).

הַשַּׁ֛חַר. Subject of temporal clause.

לַֽמָּחֳרָ֖ת. Temporal use of the preposition.

וַתַּ֥ךְ אֶת־הַקִּֽיקָי֖וֹן. Narrative discourse—mainline.

וַתַּ֥ךְ. Hiph *wayyiqtol* 3 f s from נָכָה. The subject of the verb is anaphoric, referring back to the direct object of the first clause in the verse (תּוֹלַעַת).

אֶת־הַקִּיקָיוֹן. Direct object of וַתַּךְ.

וַיִּיבָשׁ. Narrative discourse—mainline. Qal *wayyiqtol* 3 m s. The subject of the verb is הַקִּיקָיוֹן, which functioned as the direct object in the previous clause. A *wayyiqtol* that follows another *wayyiqtol* may signify a consequential (as opposed to merely sequential) situation (WO, 558–59).

Jonah 4:8-11

[8]Now when the sun rose, God appointed a cutting east wind and the sun struck the head of Jonah so that he was faint and begged to die. Then he said, "My death is preferable to my life." [9]And then God said to Jonah, "Is it right for you to be angry concerning the plant?" And he said, "It is right for me to be angry enough to die." [10]Then the LORD said, "You yourself had pity on the plant, which you did not toil over it and you did not make it grow great, which arose in a night and perished in a night. [11]But shall I not have pity upon Nineveh, the great city, which there is in it more than 120,000 humans who do not know their right hand from their left and many cattle?"

4:8 וַיְהִי | כִּזְרֹחַ הַשֶּׁמֶשׁ וַיְמַן אֱלֹהִים רוּחַ קָדִים
חֲרִישִׁית וַתַּךְ הַשֶּׁמֶשׁ עַל־רֹאשׁ יוֹנָה וַיִּתְעַלָּף
וַיִּשְׁאַל אֶת־נַפְשׁוֹ לָמוּת וַיֹּאמֶר טוֹב מוֹתִי מֵחַיָּי:

וַיְהִי כִּזְרֹחַ הַשֶּׁמֶשׁ. Narrative discourse—off-the-line. Although וַיְהִי is a *wayyiqtol*, the verb functions as a transition marker, indicating a new scene or episode in the narrative.

וַיְהִי. Qal *wayyiqtol* 3 m s.

כְּזְרֹחַ. Prep + Qal inf constr. When וַיְהִי is followed by a כְּ + infinitive construct, the phrase is intended to connote the temporal proximity of two events on a time line. Further, "these constructions are often used at the climax of a scene in order to signal what triggered a climactic event" (MNK, 332). The events in verse 8, while connected thematically and verbally to the preceding events, look forward towards the climactic event—the speech of God in verses 10-11.

הַשֶּׁמֶשׁ. Subject of infinitive construct (כְּזְרֹחַ).

וַיְמַן אֱלֹהִים רוּחַ קָדִים חֲרִישִׁית. Narrative discourse—mainline.

וַיְמַן. See 4:6.

אֱלֹהִים. The verb מָנָה appears four times in Jonah (2:1; 4:6; 4:7; 4:8), with the subject of the verb being the deity, yet in each case a slight variation in the name occurs. In 2:1, יְהוָה appears. In 4:6, it is יְהוָה אֱלֹהִים, while in 4:7, אֱלֹהִים appears with the definite article. The final appearance of the verb in 4:8 simply has אֱלֹהִים.

רוּחַ קָדִים. The direct object may be termed an "effected object," in that the object is the product of the action, and did not exist prior to the action of the verb. The absolute noun functions attributively in the construct phrase.

חֲרִישִׁית. The adjective is a *hapax legomenon*, whose meaning has proven difficult to determine with any certainty. חָרַשׁ (II) is frequently considered the root, thus translating it as a "gentle" or "still" wind (cf. Targum Jonathan). But this rendering appears unsatisfactory given the larger context. The LXX has συγκαιοντι ("scorching"), which does seem to resonate with the remainder of the chapter, perhaps alluding to the scorching sirocco that comes from the desert (Wolff, 171). Sasson has proposed, based on the frequent word plays in chapter 4, that the author may have chosen חָרַשׁ because of its similarity with שַׁחַר in the previous verse. Yet Sasson notes both Jonah 1:4 and Exodus 14:21 where synonyms of "powerful" appear to modify "wind." As a result, he avers that the unfamiliar term חֲרִישִׁית should be considered another synonym of "powerful" as well. Another and perhaps more basic proposal is that the adjective is related to a different root חָרַשׁ, meaning "to plough," "cut," or "stab." As a result, the implication would be that it was a "cutting" east wind.

וַתַּךְ הַשֶּׁמֶשׁ עַל־רֹאשׁ יוֹנָה. Narrative discourse—mainline.

וַתַּךְ. Hiph *wayyiqtol* 3 f s from נָכָה. Wolff contends that when נָכָה appears with the sun as its subject, the notion is that of a sun-stroke (Wolff, 172). Such a rendering appears supported in Psalm 121:6 and Isaiah 49:10. In addition, such an understanding might contribute further to Jonah's plea to die at the end of the verse.

הַשֶּׁמֶשׁ. Subject of וַתַּךְ.

עַל־רֹאשׁ יוֹנָה. The preposition is understood locationally, with the prepositional phrase functioning as an adjunct to the verb.

וַיִּתְעַלָּף. Narrative discourse—mainline. Hithpael *wayyiqtol* 3 m s. Rather than rendering the *wayyiqtol* as sequential, it is probably best understood as consequential. The verb indicates a consequence of the previous act. Thus, rather than translating the verb "and then he became faint," the meaning might be better rendered, "so that he became faint."

וַיִּשְׁאַל אֶת־נַפְשׁוֹ לָמוּת. Narrative discourse—mainline.

וַיִּשְׁאַל. Qal *wayyiqtol* 3 m s. The verb שָׁאַל can refer to a situation in which the "outcome of the request is so tenuous that the lexeme weakens to making a prayerful wish" (Beck, 8). In some contexts, this might best be understood as an act of begging (Ps 109:10). The exact phrase also appears in the Elijah narratives (1 Kgs 19:4), thus suggesting the narrator's continued use of the Elijah tradition in Jonah.

אֶת־נַפְשׁוֹ. Nouns such as נֶפֶשׁ and לֵבָב with pronominal suffixes may be used to express a reflexive relationship ("himself").

לָמוּת. The infinitive construct serves as a verbal complement meant to complete the thought of the main verb in the clause.

וַיֹּאמֶר. Narrative discourse—mainline. On the role of אָמַר as a discourse switch cue, see 1:6. Qal *wayyiqtol* 3 m s.

טוֹב מוֹתִי מֵחַיָּי. Embedded expository discourse—mainline. The events that have preceded the final clause in verse 8 lead up to a shift in discourse (from narrative to expository), yielding the central thought of Jonah in a verbless clause. On the nature of the comparative structure of the clause, see 4:3.

4:9   וַיֹּאמֶר אֱלֹהִים אֶל־יוֹנָה הַהֵיטֵב חָרָה־לְךָ עַל־
הַקִּיקָיוֹן וַיֹּאמֶר הֵיטֵב חָרָה־לִי עַד־מָוֶת:

וַיֹּאמֶר אֱלֹהִים אֶל־יוֹנָה. Narrative discourse—mainline. On the role of אמר as a discourse switch cue, see 1:6.

וַיֹּאמֶר. Qal *wayyiqtol* 3 m s.

אֱלֹהִים. Subject of וַיֹּאמֶר.

אֶל־יוֹנָה. The prepositional phrase functions as an adjunct to the verb, marking out the goal of the saying process

הַהֵיטֵב חָרָה־לְךָ עַל־הַקִּיקָיוֹן. Embedded expository discourse—off-the-line. On the function of the X + *qatal* construction, see 4:4.

הַהֵיטֵב. Inter + Hiph inf abs. On the use of interrogatives to mark a clause as rhetorical, see 4:4. On the function of the inf abs in such a construction, see 4:4.

חָרָה־לְךָ. Qal *qatal* 3 m s. On the impersonal construction in Hebrew, see 4:2.

עַל־הַקִּיקָיוֹן. The preposition indicates specification of topic.

וַיֹּאמֶר. Narrative discourse—mainline. On the role of אָמַר as a discourse switch cue, see 1:6. Qal *wayyiqtol* 3 m s.

הֵיטֵב חָרָה־לִי עַד־מָוֶת. Embedded expository discourse—off-the-line. On the function of the X + *qatal* construction in the same clause, see 4:4.

הֵיטֵב. Hiph inf abs. In 4:4, an interrogative precedes the verb. Its absence here highlights the rhetoric of Jonah in response to God's initial question in 4:4.

חָרָה־לִי. Qal *qatal* 3 m s + prep + 1 c s suffix. On the impersonal construction in Hebrew, see 4:2.

עַד־מָוֶת. The preposition typically expresses the measure or degree of the noun ("enough to die"). The prepositional phrase, however, does not appear elsewhere in Scripture and should probably be taken as hyperbolic (Sasson, 307) or as an unusual superlative construction (Wolff, 172). Jonah's question is nearly identical to that of God's (הַהֵיטֵב חָרָה־לְךָ עַל־הַקִּיקָיוֹן). In addition to omitting the interrogative ה, the narrator replaces עַל־הַקִּיקָיוֹן with עַד־מָוֶת, further intensifying the response.

4:10 וַיֹּאמֶר יְהוָה אַתָּה חַסְתָּ עַל־הַקִּיקָיוֹן אֲשֶׁר לֹא־
עָמַלְתָּ בּוֹ וְלֹא גִדַּלְתּוֹ שֶׁבִּן־לַיְלָה הָיָה וּבִן־לַיְלָה
אָבָד׃

וַיֹּאמֶר יְהוָה. Narrative discourse—mainline. On the role of אמר as a discourse switch cue, see 1:6. Speech formulas that include the subject but fail to indicate the recipient (unspecified recipient) typically appear in locations where there is a speaker-centered outburst of emotion, or where the speaker intends to close the dialog (Longacre, 184; Rocine, 354).

וַיֹּאמֶר. Qal *wayyiqtol* 3 m s.

יְהוָה. Subject of וַיֹּאמֶר.

אַתָּה חַסְתָּ עַל־הַקִּיקָיוֹן. Embedded expository discourse—off-the-line. The clause introduces an oral narrative discourse embedded within the larger expository discourse (Rocine, 150).

אַתָּה. The X + *qatal* construction in the present clause stands in contrast with the X + *qatal* construction at the beginning of verse 11. In both cases, a "redundant" (pleonastic) pronoun is followed by the same finite verb (חוס). The "redundant" pronoun allows for a comparison between Jonah's treatment of הַקִּיקָיוֹן and God's response to Nineveh (on the use of redundant pronouns, see Bandstra, 122).

חַסְתָּ. Qal *qatal* 2 m s from חוס.

עַל־הַקִּיקָיוֹן. The preposition indicates specification of topic.

אֲשֶׁר לֹא־עָמַלְתָּ בּוֹ וְלֹא גִדַּלְתּוֹ. Embedded expository discourse—off-the-line. The relative clause provides background information for the mainline. Although the clause continues the oral narrative discourse, the appearance of לֹא converts both verbs to irrealis, offering a statement of what did not happen, rather than a statement of what occurred.

אֲשֶׁר. Relative pronoun. The antecedent to the relative pronoun is הַקִּיקָיוֹן, and operates as the object of the relative clause. The antecedent to the relative pronoun is referred to by the pronominal suffixes that appear later in the clause (בּוֹ and גִדַּלְתּוֹ). The pronouns are understood as "resumptive elements" within the clause.

לֹא־עָמַלְתָּ. Neg + Qal *qatal* 2 m s.

בּוֹ. Although relatively rare, the preposition בְּ can mark the direct object of a verb (cf. Deut 7:7), thus making the entire prepositional phrase a complement to the verb. Objective pronoun.

וְלֹא גִדַּלְתּוֹ. *Waw* cop + neg + Piel *qatal* 2 m s + 3 m s. On the factitive sense of the Piel, see AC, 41–44 (see also WO, 400–404). The pronoun serves as the direct object of the verb.

הָיָ֤ה וּבִן־לַ֙יְלָה֙ אָבָ֔ד שֶׁבִּן־לַ֖יְלָה. Embedded expository discourse—off-the-line. *Qatals* in a dependent clause provide background information.

שֶׁבִּן־לַ֖יְלָה. The antecedent to the relative pronoun operates as the subject of the relative clause. The relative clause is marked, with בִּן־לַ֖יְלָה fronted, further contrasting the claim of this relative clause with the previous relative clause (אֲשֶׁ֤ר לֹא־עָמַ֙לְתָּ֙ בּ֔וֹ וְלֹ֥א גִדַּלְתּֽוֹ).

הָיָ֤ה. Qal *qatal* 3 m s.

וּבִן־לַ֖יְלָה. On the fronting of the phrase, see above.

אָבָ֔ד. Qal *qatal* 3 m s. Note that אָבַד ("to perish") is semantically opposite to the first verb in the clause, הָיָה ("to become").

4:11 וַאֲנִי֙ לֹ֣א אָח֔וּס עַל־נִֽינְוֵ֖ה הָעִ֣יר הַגְּדוֹלָ֑ה אֲשֶׁ֣ר יֶשׁ־
בָּ֡הּ הַרְבֵּה֩ מִֽשְׁתֵּים־עֶשְׂרֵ֨ה רִבּ֜וֹ אָדָ֗ם אֲשֶׁ֤ר לֹֽא־יָדַע֙
בֵּין־יְמִינ֣וֹ לִשְׂמֹאל֔וֹ וּבְהֵמָ֖ה רַבָּֽה׃

וַאֲנִי֙ לֹ֣א אָח֔וּס עַל־נִֽינְוֵ֖ה הָעִ֣יר הַגְּדוֹלָ֑ה. Embedded expository discourse—off-the-line. The verse opens with an X + *yiqtol* construction.

וַאֲנִי֙. Disjunctive *waw* + 1 c s. On the use of the redundant pronoun for contrast, see 4:10.

לֹ֣א אָח֔וּס. Neg + Qal *yiqtol* 1 c s. Although no interrogative is present, the context of the verse, its link with the previous verse by way of disjunctive *waw*, as well as the use of a *yiqtol*, all suggest that the sentence is best understood as a rhetorical question (Wolff, 161).

עַל־נִֽינְוֵ֖ה. The preposition indicates specification of topic.

הָעִ֣יר הַגְּדוֹלָ֑ה. The noun stands in apposition to נִֽינְוֵה. Attributive use of the adjective.

אֲשֶׁר יֶשׁ־בָּהּ הַרְבֵּה מִשְׁתֵּים־עֶשְׂרֵה רִבּוֹ אָדָם. Embedded expository discourse—off-the-line. Relative clause meant to modify נִינְוֵה הָעִיר הַגְּדוֹלָה.

אֲשֶׁר. Relative pronoun. On the use of the antecedent to the relative pronoun as the subject of the subordinate clause, see 4:10.

יֶשׁ־בָּהּ. The particle of existence frequently signals a mainline construction in expository discourse, but given the presence of the relative pronoun, the clause must be understood as dependent, and hence off-the-line. The preposition בְּ indicates spatial localization—the so-called *beth locale*.

הַרְבֵּה. Hiph inf abs. Functioning substantively as the subject of the verbless clause.

מִשְׁתֵּים־עֶשְׂרֵה רִבּוֹ. Comparative use of the preposition מִן, "more than."

אָדָם. Collective noun.

אֲשֶׁר לֹא־יָדַע בֵּין־יְמִינוֹ לִשְׂמֹאלוֹ. Embedded expository discourse—off-the-line. A *qatal* in a dependent clause provides background or explanatory information.

אֲשֶׁר. Relative pronoun. The antecedent to the relative pronoun (אָדָם) serves as the subject of the subordinate clause,

לֹא־יָדַע. Neg + Qal *qatal* 3 m s.

בֵּין־יְמִינוֹ לִשְׂמֹאלוֹ. The phrase יָדַע בֵּין . . . לְ functions idiomatically, meaning "to distinguish" (Wolff, 175).

וּבְהֵמָה רַבָּה. The noun may be understood as a defective clause, in that it is not actually a clause itself, but instead, the second part of a complex verbless clause (אֲשֶׁר יֶשׁ־בָּהּ הַרְבֵּה מִשְׁתֵּים־עֶשְׂרֵה רִבּוֹ אָדָם), which was interrupted by the previous relative clause. For a similar construction, see 1:5.

GLOSSARY

adjunct—At the syntactic level, the term refers to non-verbal elements that can be removed from the predicate without disrupting the grammatical construction.

anaphora—a grammatical element that references another word that appeared earlier in the text.

apocopation—the shortening of a word at the end (often the dropping of a final guttural), resulting in changes to the syllable structure.

apposition—the placement of two nouns in juxtaposition, with one noun serving as a descriptive or explanatory modifier to the head. The noun in apposition has the same syntactic function as the head noun.

asyndetic—the coordination of nouns or clauses without normal coordinating or subordinating conjunctions.

cataphora—a grammatical element that points forward to other words that appear in a sentence or unit.

complement—At the syntactic level, the term refers to obligatory, non-omissible, and non-verbal parts of the predicate that complete the verb. Direct objects and indirect objects are two examples of complements.

complementizer—a word or phrase used to mark reported speech or another clause.

deixis—a system of words that shift in reference, depending upon the speech situation (he/she; this/that; now/then).

dependent clause—*see* subordinate clause.

diaphora—the repetition of a word in a discourse, where the meaning of the word has shifted slightly with each occurrence.

direct object—a noun that receives the action of a transitive verb.

discourse switch cue—a word or grammatical construction used to signal the reader that the discourse has changed.

double entendre—a word or phrase used by the author with the intention of invoking multiple levels of meaning in the mind of the reader.

embedding—the placement of one type of discourse within another type of discourse.

epexegetical—the function of clarifying preceding material.

fronting—the placement of a clausal constituent before the verb (ex., "from before the Lord, he was fleeing," Jonah 1:10).

indirect object—a noun that receives the direct object in a clause.

intransitive—a verb that does not take a direct object.

jussive—a volitional expression that conveys a wish or indirect command in the *yiqtol* third or second person. With weak verbs, the jussive may appear apocopated.

merismus—a poetic device in which an idea is alluded to by reference to its two parts, often expressed in opposite terms. For example, when the psalmist speaks of meditating on God's word "day and night" (Ps 1:2), he refers to the larger concept of "continually" meditating.

pleonasm—the unnecessary use of a grammatical element, resulting in redundancy.

semantics—the study of the meaning of words.

stative verb—a verb that describes a state of being rather than an event involving action (קָטֹן).

subordinate clause—any clause that stands in relationship to an independent clause. Also referred to as a dependent clause.

syntax—the term refers to the study of clauses and sentences in a language, with particular attention given to the formal connections and relationships that exist between the elements found therein.

topicalization—refers to a focus-shifting device in which new information is placed in a location where given information is usually found.

waw copulative—the normal conjunction (וְ) that is prefixed to any word to connect words, phrases, or clauses. Also known as the "waw conjunction." The waw copulative has no semantic value, other than that of "and."

BIBLIOGRAPHY

Allen, Leslie C. *The Books of Joel, Obadiah, Jonah and Micah.* The New International Commentary on the Old Testament. Grand Rapids: Eerdmans, 1976.

Arnold, Bill and John H. Choi. *A Guide to Biblical Hebrew Syntax.* Cambridge: Cambridge University, 2003.

Auffret, Pierre. "Pivot Pattern: nouveaux exemples (Jon 2:10; Ps 31:13; Is 23:7)." *Vetus Testamentum* 28 (1978): 103–10.

Bandstra, Barry. "Word Order and Emphasis in Biblical Hebrew Narrative." Pages 109–23 in *Linguistics and Biblical Hebrew.* Edited by W. R. Bodine. Winona Lake, Ind.: Eisenbrauns, 1992.

Barré, Michael L. "Jonah 2:9 and the Structure of Jonah's Prayer." *Biblica* 72 (1991): 237–48.

Beck, John A. "שׁאל." Pages 7–10. In *New International Dictionary of Old Testament Theology and Exegesis*, vol. 4. Edited by Willem A. Van Gemeren. Grand Rapids: Zondervan, 1997.

Berlin, Adele. *The Dynamics of Biblical Parallelism.* Bloomington: Indiana University, 1985.

Bodine, Walter R. "Linguistics and Philology in the Study of Ancient Near Eastern Languages." Pages 39–54 in *Working With No Data: Semitic and Egyptian Studies Presented to Thomas O. Lambdin.* Edited by Thomas O. Lambdin, David M. Golomb and Susan T. Hollis. 1987. Winona Lake, Ind.: Eisenbrauns, 1987.

Buth, Randall. "Word Order in the Verbless Clause: A Generative Functional Approach." Pages 79–108 in *The Verbless Clause in Biblical Hebrew.* Edited by Cynthia Miller. Winona Lake, Ind.: Eisenbrauns, 1999.

Christensen, Duane L. "The Song of Jonah: A Metrical Analysis." *Journal of Biblical Literature* 104 (1985): 217–31.

Craig, Kenneth M., Jr. "Jonah and the Reading Process." *Journal for the Study of the Old Testament* 47 (1990): 103–14.

Crenshaw, James L. "The Expression *mî yôdea* in the Hebrew Bible." *Vetus Testamentum* 36 (1986): 274–88.

Cross, Frank M. "Studies in the Structure of Hebrew Verse: The Prosody of the Psalm of Jonah." Pages 159–67 in *The Quest for the Kingdom of God: Studies in Honor of George E. Mendenhall.* Edited by George E. Mendendall, H. B. Huffmon, F. A. Spina and Alberto R. W. Green. 1983. Winona Lake, Ind.: Eisenbrauns, 1983.

Crouch, Walter B. "To Question an End, to End a Question: Opening the Closure of the Book of Jonah." *Journal for the Study of the Old Testament* 62 (1994): 101–12.

Culy, Martin. *I, II, III John.* Waco, Tex.: Baylor University, 2004.

Dahood, Mitchell J. "Independent personal pronoun in the oblique case in Hebrew." *Catholic Biblical Quarterly* 32 (1970): 86–90.

Dawson, David A. *Text-Linguistics and Biblical Hebrew.* Journal for the Study of the Old Testament Supplement 177. Sheffield: Sheffield Academic, 1994.

Domeris, W. R. "סַפְן." Pages 281–82 in the *New International Dictionary of Old Testament Theology and Exegesis*, vol. 3. Edited by Willem A. Van Gemeren. Grand Rapids: Zondervan, 1997.

Freedman, David N. "Jonah 1:4b." *Journal of Biblical Literature* 77 (1958): 161–62.

Garr, W. R. "The Qinah : A Study of Poetic Meter, Syntax, and Style." *Zeitschrift für die alttestamentliche Wissenschaft* 95 (1983): 54–75.

Garrett, Duane A. *A Modern Grammar for Classical Hebrew.* Nashville: Broadman & Holman, 2002.

Harman, Allan M. "נפל." Pages 129–31 in the *New International Dictionary of Old Testament Theology and Exegesis*, vol. 3. Edited by Willem A. Van Gemeren. Grand Rapids: Zondervan, 1997.

Holbert, John C. "'Deliverance Belongs to Yahweh:' Satire in the Book of Jonah." *Journal for the Study of the Old Testament* 21 (1981): 59–81.

Hollady, William, ed. *A Concise Hebrew and Aramaic Lexicon of the Old Testament.* Grand Rapids: Eerdmans, 1988.

Horwitz, William J. "Another Interpretation of Jonah 1:12." *Vetus Testamentum* 23 (1973): 370–72.

Houk, Cornelius B. "Linguistic Patterns in Jonah." *Journal for the Study of the Old Testament* 77 (1998): 81–102.

Joüon, Paul. *A Grammar of Biblical Hebrew.* Translated and revised by T. Muraoka. 2 vols. Subsidia Biblica 14. Rome: Pontifical Institute, 1993.

Kamp, Albert H. *Inner Worlds: A Cognitive Linguistic Approach to the Book of Jonah.* Leiden: Brill, 2004.

Kautzsch, Emil, ed. *Gesenius' Hebrew Grammar.* Translated and revised by A. E. Cowley. 2nd English edition. Oxford: Clarendon, 1910.

Limburg, James. *Jonah.* Old Testament Library. Louisville: Westminster John Knox, 1993.

Longacre, Robert E. *Joseph: A Story of Divine Providence.* Winona Lake, Ind.: Eisenbrauns, 1989.

Longacre, Robert E. "Discourse Perspective on the Hebrew Verb: Affirmation and Restatement." Pages 177–89 in *Linguistics and Biblical Hebrew*. Edited by Walter R. Bodine. Winona Lake, Ind.: Eisenbrauns, 1992.

Longacre, Robert E. and Shin Ja J. Hwang. "A Textlinguistic Approach to the Biblical Hebrew Narrative of Jonah." Pages 336–58 in *Biblical Hebrew and Discourse Linguistics*. Edited by Robert Bergen. Winona Lake, Ind.: Eisenbrauns, 1994.

Magonet, Jonathan. *Form and Meaning: Studies in Literary Techniques in the Book of Jonah*. Beiträge zur biblischen Exegese und Theologie 2. Frankfort: Peter Lang, 1976.

Miller, Cynthia. *The Representation of Speech in Biblical Hebrew Narrative: A Linguistic Analysis*. Harvard Semitic Monographs 55. Winona Lake, Ind.: Eisenbrauns, 2003.

Miller, Cynthia, ed. *The Verbless Clause in Biblical Hebrew*. Winona Lake, Ind.: Eisenbrauns, 1999.

Niccacci, Alviero. *The Syntax of the Verb in Classical Hebrew Prose*. Journal for the Study of the Old Testament Supplement Series 86. Translated by W. G. E. Watson. Sheffield: Sheffield Academic, 1990.

———. "Syntactic Analysis of Jonah." *Linguistic Analysis* 46 (1996): 9-32.

Rocine, Bryan M. *Learning Biblical Hebrew: A New Approach Using Discourse Analysis*. Macon, Ga.: Smyth & Helwys, 2000.

Sasson, Jack M. *Jonah*. Anchor Bible 24B. New York: Doubleday, 1990.

Simon, Uriel. Jonah. *The JPS Bible Commentary*. Philadelphia: The Jewish Publication Society, 1999.

Sinclair, Cameron. "Are Nominal Clauses a Distinct Clausal Type?" Pages 51–75 in *The Verbless Clause in Biblical Hebrew*. Edited by Cynthia Miller. Winona Lake: Eisenbrauns, 1999.

Snaith, Norman H. *Notes on the Hebrew Text of the Book of Jonah*. London: Epworth, 1945.

Trible, Phyllis. *Rhetorical Criticism: Context, Method, and the Book of Jonah*. Guides to Biblical Scholarship. Minneapolis: Fortress, 1994.

Van der Merwe, Christo H. J., Jackie A. Naudé, and Jan H. Kroeze. *A Biblical Hebrew Reference Grammar*. Biblical Languages: Hebrew 3. Sheffield: Sheffield Academic. 1999.

Van Woulde, Ellen. "Linguistic Motivation and Biblical Exegesis." Pages 21–50 in *Narrative Syntax and the Hebrew Bible*. Edited by Ellen van Woulde. Boston: Brill, 2002.

————, ed. *Narrative Syntax and the Hebrew Bible*. Boston: Brill, 2002.

Waltke, Bruce K. and Michael O'Connor. *An Introduction to Biblical Hebrew Syntax*. Winona Lake, Ind.: Eisenbrauns, 1990.

Walsh, Jerome T. "Jonah 2:3-10: A Rhetorical Critical Study." *Biblica* 63 (1982): 219–29.

Watson, Wilfred G. E. *Classical Hebrew Poetry: A Guide to Its Techniques*. Journal for the Study of the Old Testament Supplement 26. Sheffield: JSOT Press, 1984.

Wendland, Ernst R. "The Discourse Analysis of Hebrew Poetry: A Procedural Outline." Pages 1–27 in *Discourse Perspectives on Hebrew Poetry in the Scriptures*. Edited by E. R. Wendlend. New York: United Bible Society, 1994.

————. "Recursion and Variation in the 'Prophecy' of Jonah: On the Rhetorical Impact of Stylistic Technique in Hebrew Narrative Discourse, with Special Reference to Irony and Enigma." *Andrews University Seminary Studies* 35 (1997): 189–209.

———. "Text Analysis and the Genre of Jonah." *Journal of the Evangelical Theological Society* 39 (1996): 373–95.

West, Mona. "Irony in the Book of Jonah: Audience Identification with the Hero." *Perspectives in Religious Studies* 11 (1984): 233–42.

Wolff, Hans Walter. *Jonah: A Commentary.* Translated by Margaret Kohl. Minneapolis: Augsburg, 1986.

Zevit, Ziony. *The Anterior Construction in Classical Hebrew.* Society of Biblical Literature Dissertation Series 50. Atlanta: Scholars, 1998.

AUTHOR AND SUBJECT INDEX

Note: Representative examples of specific grammatical features appear below.